BREAKING THE BOOZE HABIT:

USING "SEINFELD'S CHAIN" TO CUT DOWN HABITUAL DRINKING

BY HEATHER SHEARER PhD

Copyright © 2017 Heather Shearer

All rights reserved.

ISBN:1974342662

ISBN-13:9781974342662

DEDICATION

I'd like to dedicate this book to my family, and particularly to my sister Jill, who beat her addiction to alcohol and has been sober for many years. Go girl! You are awesome and an inspiration.

CONTENTS

CHAPTER 1: INTRODUCTION   2

Breaking the booze habit 2
    Jerry Seinfeld's Chain   5

CHAPTER 2: HOW ALCOHOL AFFECTS YOUR BODY---AND THE BENEFITS OF CUTTING DOWN OR GIVING UP ENTIRELY   7

Safe drinking: so how much is too much?   8
    So what *IS* a standard drink, or one Alcohol Unit (AU)?   8

What happens when you have a drink of alcohol?   10

Physical 11
    Heart (cardiovascular system)   12
    Liver and Pancreas   13
    Cancer   14
    Women's Health   14
    Weight gain   15
    Other health issues   17
    Accidents   17
    Sleep 18
    Brain and mental health   19
    Addiction   21

Financial   21

Spiritual 22

But what about the benefits?   23
    Substitutes for Alcohol 24
    Dealing with social pressure   25

CHAPTER 3: THE SCIENCE OF HABIT AND BEHAVIOUR CHANGE   27

The physiological basis of habit formation 27

Human instinct and how the brain creates habits   28
    Why the brain likes to form habits (it needs LOTS of energy)   31
    Rewiring the brain, or, are habits just instinct?   33

CHAPTER 4 THE PSYCHOLOGICAL BASIS OF HABIT FORMATION 40

Introduction   40
    Associative vs Script-Based   40
    Repetition, Automaticity and Stability   42
    The complexity of behaviour   47

CHAPTER 5 – THE PSYCHOLOGY OF CHANGING HABITUAL BEHAVIOUR 49

How DO you change your behaviour?   51
    Information Campaigns 53
    Comfort, cleanliness and cost   60
    Incentive and disincentive.   63
    Vigilant control   65
    Mindfulness   67

CHAPTER 5 – OVERVIEW OF HABIT FORMATION AND HABIT BREAKING TECHNIQUES 71

Five Steps to Breaking a Bad Habit 72

Five Stages of Habit Formation   74
    The rule of three   78
    False memories   80
    Using Triggers to Break Habits   81

CHAPTER SIX: LET'S PUT IT ALL TOGETHER---THE TECHNIQUE 85

Introduction   85
    Identify the habit you want to break and why it's a habit   86
    YOUR journal   87
    How I finally gave up drinking   89

CHAPTER 7 THE TECHNIQUE   99

Breaking the habit of habitual drinking   99

The Stuff.   101
- The Calendar   101
- Stickers   102
- Examples of giving up other types of bad habits   104
- Examples of some Good Habits (and mini goals)   109
- Hints and tips   113
- Incentives   113

How does it work (back to the science)   114
- Neuroscience   114
- Psychology   115

CHAPTER 8 WHEN THINGS GO WRONG   120
- Analyse (don't criticise)   120
- How to deal with cravings   122
- Consistency   123

APPENDICES 124

APPENDIX 1 Resources   124

Tests   124

REFERENCES 125

QUOTE

"Your beliefs become your thoughts,
Your thoughts become your words,
Your words become your actions,
Your actions become your habits,
Your habits become your values,
Your values become your destiny."

MAHATMA GANDHI.

CHAPTER 1: INTRODUCTION

"The chains of habit are too weak to be felt until they are too strong to be broken." — **Samuel Johnson**

BREAKING THE BOOZE HABIT

Most of us have one (or more) bad habits that we'd like to change or get rid of entirely. But even if we don't like something we do, it's very hard to DO something about it. It's so easy to procrastinate.

But one day, something triggers the motivation to **DO something**. It can be waking up with yet another hangover, or the desire to really stick to a New Year's resolution, or maybe it's the zip on your favourite jeans finally giving up.

So we enthusiastically launch into action to break a habit such as drinking. This is particularly common at certain times of year; New Year's resolutions, FebFast, Dry July, Ocsober, or after a music festival or holiday.

And usually, we can do it, for a couple of days, even weeks. But it is all too common to lapse. We love to make excuses to have a drink, or other habit, such as a cigarette, saying to ourselves, 'it's just one', or 'I'll give up after the rellies leave', or we sleep in instead of going to the gym—'---but, it doesn't matter---I'll definitely start again tomorrow'. But we all know that 'tomorrow never comes'.

But why do so many of us manage to quit habits in the short term and then start again? Why can we give up alcohol for a few days or weeks, and then lapse? Why is it that nearly all people who lose weight put it back on again? What about other bad habits, like smoking, or not exercising, or gambling or spending too long on the internet?

This is because all of these can be deeply engrained **HABITS**---and habits can be extremely resistant to change.

This book is aimed at those of us who feel that we enjoy a drink, but perhaps a little too much. Maybe we've transitioned from an occasional social drink, to a glass of wine every night, or from one glass to two or three. Maybe we want to quit drinking entirely, or maybe we just want to cut down a bit.

But most of us have tried many times to change. And many of us have failed.

Well, I've got a way to achieve lasting change.

> **Please note however that this book is not aimed at those with a serious medical problem,** such as drug or alcohol addiction, or if you are extremely overweight. This book is aimed at breaking **minor habits**, such as drinking a little bit too much (say, an extra glass here or there) If your issue is more severe, please consider consulting a medical practitioner, psychologist or counsellor. You CAN use the technique to reduce drinking or other habits like smoking or snacking in the evening.

In this book, I share a simple and cheap technique that you can use to break bad habits. The book is primarily focused on cutting down or giving up drinking, but you can use it for any bad habit that you wish to modify or break. It's based on the latest psychological research and aims to help in breaking habits that make you unhappy or creating new and better habits.

That's important. Not everyone will see the same habits as 'bad', but everyone has some habits they don't like. Most techniques that aim to break bad habits are difficult to maintain, and often based on flawed or incorrect interpretations of the science. I'm not a journalist or trying to sell something (apart from this book of course), but am a university researcher, studying behavioural psychology and environmental science. I'd like to share some insights that I've gained from my own and other's research. My doctorate was on environmental behaviour and behavioural psychology, but the underlying principles are the same.

I've also spent much of my life trying to break various bad habits, without much success—that was, until I began to apply some techniques from my academic life to my personal life. I also researched the whole issue of behavioural change, and habits, why they form, how people successfully break habits and how they maintain their new lifestyle in the long term. I am a university researcher, and have myself successfully quit drinking, so I decided to write this book, so that hopefully, it could help other people too.

I'd like to **share with you** how I did this, and the simple techniques I used to achieve this. This book is the result of my research.

BREAKING THE BOOZE HABIT

Why did I drink?

You know those social media things that go around, saying "if you could give your younger self one piece of advice, what would it be?" Well, mine would be, "don't start drinking alcohol".

Four decades later and I never took that advice (from my future self, or from the people around me at the time). I've had a long and tempestuous relationship with alcohol; first discovering it in my late teens (my parents rarely drink) as a panacea for extreme shyness. It just made it so easy to talk to boys, when before I would stammer and blush and say something stupid, and they would look at me as if I was from another planet, and walk away. It didn't help that I had been raised in the remote African bush, and like my rescue dog, Princess (The Terrierist) was poorly socialised, then sent to boarding school at the age of 9.

The only reason I never became an actual alcoholic is that I get terrible hangovers, and even when I was at my worst, frequently binging, the migraine headaches, nausea and diarrhea were enough to stop me drinking for 2 to 3 days.

I had given up drinking before, when I was pregnant, and once because I was the process of splitting with my first ex-husband (who never gets hangovers) so I gave up alcohol (in response to his drinking) and sex (in response to his drinking). He wasn't too happy about either.

Years went by, and I gave up every now and again, mostly for things like FebFast and Dry July, but I never really stuck at it.

After some time (approximately 40 years), I saw a pattern emerging---hey, I'm a slow learner (I obviously don't learn from experience---I've been married three times). I begin to analyse myself, and ask why did I always start drinking again? And how did I succeed in breaking some habits (like giving up smoking) and not others (like giving up wine)?

> I was really unhappy with my drinking as I felt that it was becoming too habitual (not to mention expensive). I started to use a technique based on a system of incentive and motivation that I used on my children to encourage them to do their chores. It worked wonderfully!
>
> I inadvertently discovered a method that incorporated much of the research on making and breaking habits, and that was so simple to put into practice---a technique that you can use both to break bad habits and create new good habits.
>
> Since then, I've managed to significantly moderate my drinking habit. Indeed, I have totally given up alcohol, because I felt that it just wasn't fitting in with how I wanted to live my life.

Jerry Seinfeld's Chain

I first 'invented' the technique in this book entirely by myself! It was based on something I used to do to encourage my children to do their chores, and I modified it as a habit breaking tool particularly to cut my drinking habit. However, like all 'great' ideas, I discovered that it has been used before, most famously by Jerry Seinfeld as a productivity measure[1]! Oh well, great minds think alike.

This has been the only technique that I have ever used (and believe me, I have tried them all, save anti drinking meds) that has long term success in breaking the drinking habit. Ok, I did give up drinking because I was angry with my first ex-husband, but I think that and pregnancy doesn't count.

However, because I am a researcher, I wanted to understand WHY the technique works so well, so I started investigating this. If we can understand how and why something is effective, we can also modify it for our own use. In addition, breaking habits is not quite as simple as just filling in squares on a calendar. This would be equivalent to saying the Usain Bolt is an Olympic champion sprinter because he can move his legs really fast. Sure he can, but he had years of training, a natural genetic advantage and the right mindset to become the champion he is. The pertinent point here, is the *right mindset*. If we can cultivate the right mindset, then breaking our bad habits becomes much easier. That is why I dedicate such a lot of time to the psychology of habit.

In this book

I will begin with some benefits of cutting down or giving up alcohol, and then go on to the science of habit and habit forming. I will then discuss the technique in the latter half of the book, and finish with links to some really useful resources. As this will also be published as an e-book, I will keep these updated, and link to my own website and Facebook page, where you can keep up to date.

In each chapter of this book, I discuss some aspects of changing behaviour and breaking habits. The beginning of each chapter is a general overview of each aspect, and then a more in-depth analysis. The book is designed so that you may read just the first section, the entire chapter, or skip to the technique.

Chapter two discusses some of the impacts of alcohol; physical, mental, psychological, spiritual and financial. It also details some benefits of moderate drinking, and gives a breakdown of what moderate drinking actually is (frequently a lot less than people think it is). One of the reasons that I go on about the bad effects of alcohol, is that if you can keep thinking about the real reasons why you want to give up or cut down drinking; then it helps keep motivated. Keeping thinking about things helps break habitual behaviour. We are constantly bombarded with subtle and not so subtle messages that try and motivate our behaviour (for example, that drinking is romantic and upmarket and if we drink XYZ beer or champagne, we too can be like that glamorous couple on the yacht). Of course, the glamorous couple are models who are paid to look like that. We need to be conscious of the reasons why we PERSONALLY want to do something, not what the advertisers want us to do.

Chapter three discusses the science behind behaviour change, beginning with the neurological basis of behaviour, and then finishing with the psychological aspects of behaviour.

Chapter four discusses the psychological basis of habit formation; what are some of reasons why we create habits, and why they are so hard to break.

Chapter five discusses various ways of changing behaviour (our own and others) and lists some common methods by which governments, individuals and groups try and change behaviour.

Chapter six goes into greater detail about habits; the stages of habit formation, steps to breaking habits, and the use of triggers to break habits.

Chapter seven talks about the actual technique promoted by this book and gives greater details on how to do it, how to use it for various habits, and a number of anecdotes from people who have used the technique.

The rest of the book gives links on resources, apps and other useful things you can use to help you in your habit breaking or making journey.

CHAPTER 2: HOW ALCOHOL AFFECTS YOUR BODY---AND THE BENEFITS OF CUTTING DOWN OR GIVING UP ENTIRELY

> "Once you avoid the things that accelerate aging like smoking, obesity, **excessive alcohol consumption,** and excessive sun exposure, you've done about as much as you can to influence your aging process."
> S. Jay Olshansky

We all know people who can seemingly drink without any effects at all, putting away prodigious amounts of booze. One of the best know was a famous French professional wrestler called Andre the Giant, for example, who could drink incredible amounts of alcohol, once consuming 119 cans of beer (350ml) in 6 hours (and anecdotally, more at other times, including 40 vodka shots and an entire 12 bottle case of wine in 3 hours). Not surprisingly, he died young, of congestive heart failure, aged only 47[2]. On the other hand, we all know people who can drink hardly anything and get drunk, though this is usually related to the fact that they do not drink very much to start off.

So, alcohol affects everyone differently and this is because the effect of alcohol on a person is related to things like body weight, gender, proportion of body fat, ethnicity, genetics, and of course, amount and type of alcohol consumed. Interestingly enough, if you think you are drinking alcohol (when in reality, you are just drinking a placebo) you can still act in ways that imply you have been drinking, such as exhibiting reduced judgement. A study in New Zealand showed that students drinking fake vodka flirted more, had impaired memory and even acted drunk---although they were perfectly sober![3]

Alcohol is considered a dangerous drug, but drinking is incredibly common; 55% of the world's adult population (about 3 billion people) drink alcohol. It has a long history too, humans have probably been drinking alcohol for millennia; archaeologists estimate that fermented beverages have been made

7

and drunk for at least 10,000 years[4]. Even animals drink alcohol! Elephants, birds, apes, monkeys, bats and other species all like a tipple or two[5].

Despite this, alcohol is considered to be **the most dangerous drug in the world,** in 2012 it was a direct cause of 3.3 million deaths and contributed 5.1% of the global disease burden[6].

SAFE DRINKING: SO HOW MUCH IS TOO MUCH?

Before discussing the positives and negatives of drinking, I shall detail what is considered to be safe drinking. Of note, the research on this is somewhat contested, and you may find varying information, especially on the internet (well, you find conflicting opinions on everything on the internet). Also, as mentioned previously, people are different, with different body types, genetic heritage and psychosocial backgrounds, and what is safe for one person may not be safe for another. So, this is general information only.

This is based on the Australian site, Drinkwise[7], as well as other reputable sources. Drinkwise has developed four guidelines for responsible drinking:

> 1. Reducing the risk of alcohol related harm over a lifetime
>   No more than 2 drinks (1 alcohol unit per drink, see details below) per day
> 2. Reducing the risk of injury on a single occasion of drinking
>   No more than 4 drinks on a single occasion
> 3. Children and young people under 18 years of age
>   Not drinking alcohol at all, and delay starting drinking as long as possible
> 4. Pregnancy and breastfeeding
>   Alcohol can harm the developing fetus or breastfeeding baby. Pregnant women or those planning to become pregnant should not drink at all.

So what *IS* a standard drink, or one Alcohol Unit (AU)?

This is actually quite a complicated calculation and full details of how it is calculated can be found on the Australian Government Department of Health Website[8]; however, unless you love complicated equations, as a rule of thumb, the following is an indication of ONE standard drink (with reference to Figure 2 below):

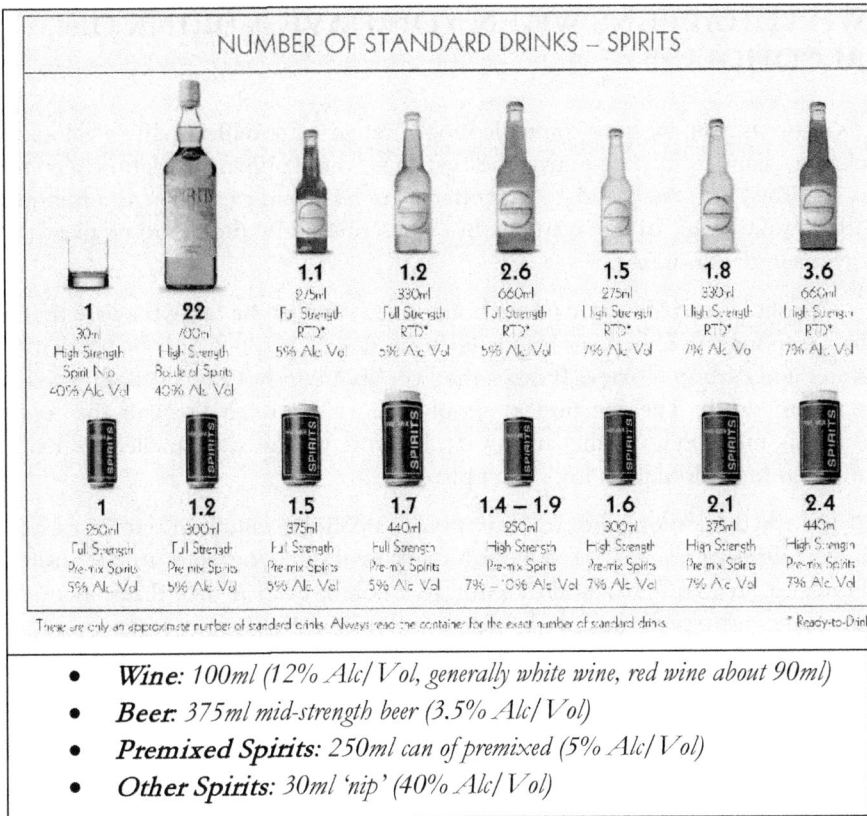

- **Wine:** 100ml (12% Alc/Vol, generally white wine, red wine about 90ml)
- **Beer:** 375ml mid-strength beer (3.5% Alc/Vol)
- **Premixed Spirits:** 250ml can of premixed (5% Alc/Vol)
- **Other Spirits:** 30ml 'nip' (40% Alc/Vol)

Figure 2; Standard Drinks Guide (source, Balranald Club[9]

Cider is similar to beer, and wine varies by the percentage of alcohol, as very heavy red wines can be around 14 or more percent. Beer (in Australia) generally ranges from light beer (around 2.7%) to heavy beer (from around 4.5% to 6%). Do be careful of some international beers, as these can be very high in alcohol, sometimes even over 10%. I once drank a South African 'light' beer on a plane, and when I felt tiddly, looked at the label, and saw that the alcohol content would have made it a heavy beer by Australian standards.

Suffice it to say, what you *think* is a standard measure of alcohol is probably a lot more than it actually IS. Most of my baby boomer friends think a 250ml wine glass is a standard measure instead of---um---2 ½ .

WHAT HAPPENS WHEN YOU HAVE A DRINK OF ALCOHOL?

As soon as you swallow some alcohol, a range of complicated physiological changes happen in your body. The first thing that happens is that the alcohol is absorbed into the blood, so that effects are felt rapidly (as soon as 5 minutes after swallowing). In this way, alcohol is distributed by the blood to all of the organs in the body[10].

Alcohol is actually toxic to the body, so as soon as the body is aware that it has been ingested, the liver begins to break down the poison, converting it to water and carbon dioxide. It takes the liver about an hour to break down one standard drink. The remainder (about 10%) is excreted through the lungs (breath), the kidneys (urine) and sweat. I'm sure you have all smelled someone who has been drinking a lot; it isn't pleasant.

As you drink more, the concentration of alcohol in your body increases, and if you drink more than a standard drink an hour, you start to get drunk. However, everyone reacts differently to alcohol, even if they drink identical amounts and types of alcohol. This is influenced by various factors such as body type, gender, age, ethnicity, liver genetics, whether you have eaten or not, speed of drinking, other health conditions, any medications you are taking, and how often you drink (if you rarely drink, you can become what is colloquially known in Australia as a 'two pot screamer' (a pot is about 275mm of beer).

The more you drink, the less the body is able to process the alcohol. As your blood alcohol concentration increase, you can start to feel ill, judgement is affected, and coordination suffers (we've all seen drunk people stumbling around or worse---trying to dance). In this state, you risk injury from falls, car crashes or walking on dangerous roads, and vulnerability to violence and sexual assault. As concentration gets higher, you can suffer blackouts.

If you continue to drink, you can actually **die** from alcohol poisoning. This means that there is so much alcohol in the bloodstream that the parts of your brain the control things like heartbeat and breathing can shut down. Breathing and heartbeat are, of course, quite important to your continued survival. Symptoms of alcohol poisoning include unconsciousness, clammy skin, vomiting, seizures, trouble with breathing and low body temperature. One of the commonest ways of dying from too much alcohol is that the gag reflex which stops you from choking is suppressed, so people can vomit and choke to death on their own vomit[11].

Also, blood alcohol levels can keep rising for some hours, so you are not necessarily safe from alcohol poisoning for some time after you stop drinking. Even if a person does not die from alcohol poisoning, they can be seriously

BREAKING THE BOOZE HABIT

and permanently brain damaged. Alcohol poisoning, unlike the chronic effects of alcohol such as cirrhosis, most often affects people who are not used to drinking to excess, such as college students.

Finally, any drinking at all whilst pregnant immediately affects the unborn fetus, as alcohol is carried around the body by the blood. Particularly at certain periods of development, alcohol can have significant and permanent negative impacts on the baby, manifesting in what is known as fetal alcohol spectrum disorder, characterised by mental retardation, growth deficiency, facial abnormalities and other problems.

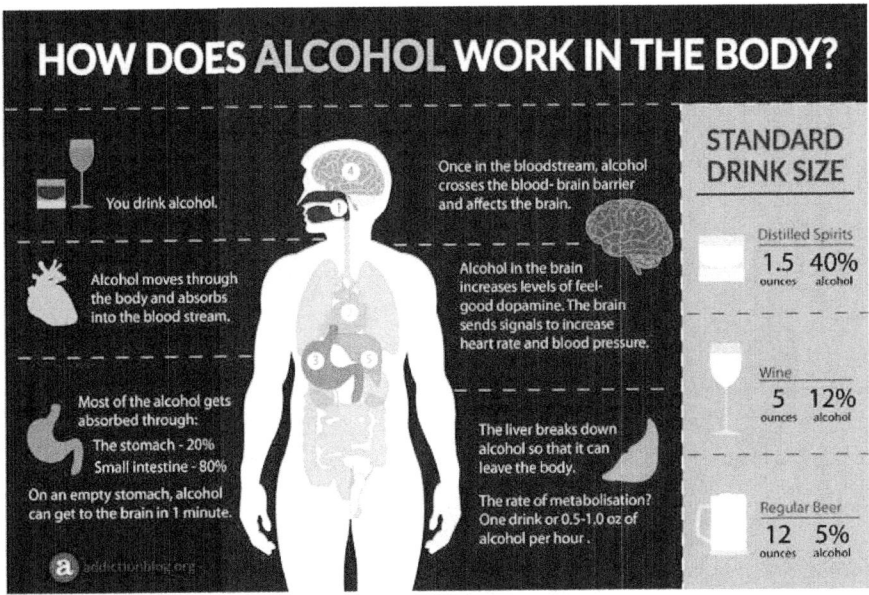

Figure 3. How Alcohol travels through the body (Source: addictionblog[12]

PHYSICAL

Much as we don't like to admit it, alcohol is a poison. It is toxic to the body and can kill you (quickly from alcohol poisoning, or slowly from diseases like cirrhosis of the liver or various cancers). Have a few drinks too many, and to most, it is obvious the next morning that you have poisoned yourself.

Alcohol impacts the heart, brain, gut, liver, pancreas, immune system, and has been implicated as a risk factor for a number of cancers (such as bowel, breast, mouth, liver and throat). It's linked to weight gain and an increase in visceral fat (the bad fat that collects around the abdomen and internal organs). When you drink, the liver stops fat burning, and burns off the alcohol instead.

BREAKING THE BOOZE HABIT

Heart (cardiovascular system)

Heart disease kills more people every year than any other cause, as can be seen in Figure 4 (and many of the other causes of death in this diagram are indirectly caused or exacerbated by alcohol). The cardiovascular system consists of the heart, blood vessels and blood. When you drink alcohol, it causes a temporary increase in heart rate and blood pressure, and in time, these short term effects can become more permanent, with other problems such as weakened heart muscles and arrhythmia (irregular heartbeats).

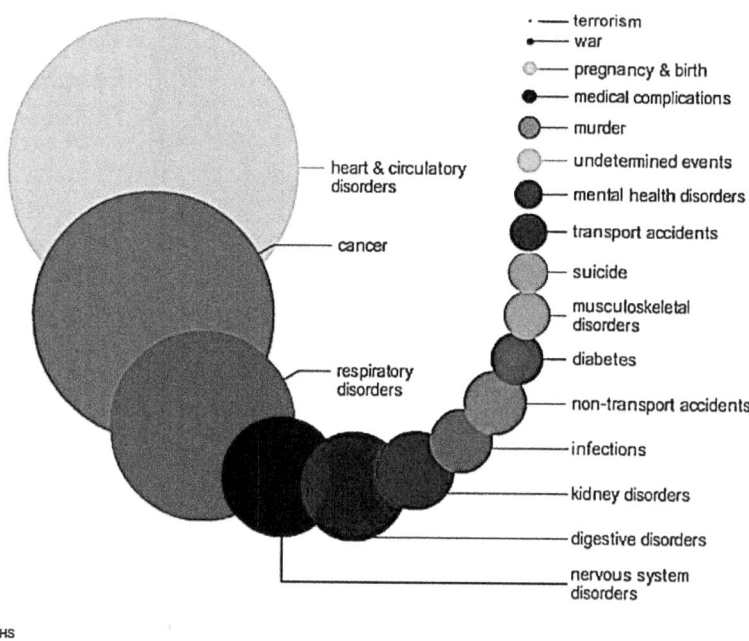

Figure 4. Source: Business Insider [13]

Increased heart rate (tachycardia) and irregular heartbeats (arrhythmias) have a number of serious impacts on health, including death from heart attacks and stroke. A common arrhythmia, atrial fibrillation or palpitations, has also been termed 'holiday heart' because it frequently occurs at times when alcohol intake is increased, such as over Christmas and New Year. More serious arrhythmias, such as ventricular fibrillation, have also been linked with excessive consumption of alcohol[14].

BREAKING THE BOOZE HABIT

Another long term impact on the heart is alcoholic cardiomyopathy, or weakened heart muscles. Over time, excessive alcohol intake weakens the heart muscle, so it cannot effectively pump blood, weakening organs and causing swollen legs and feet. Eventually the condition will lead to heart failure and may even require a heart transplant. This condition is almost completely reversible if caught in time, and the person stops drinking alcohol.

Excessive drinking, especially binge drinking, is directly responsible for many cases of high blood pressure (hypertension). Heavy drinking causes usually flexible blood vessels to become more rigid and stiff, constricting them and raising blood pressure. High blood pressure is implicated in heart disease.

Alcohol is a factor in ischemic strokes (caused by foreign bodies such as blood clots stopping the flow of blood to parts of the brain) from raising blood pressure, increasing the risk of blood clots, and from raising levels of bad cholesterol. It is also a cause of hemorrhagic strokes (arteries that supply the brain breaking or bleeding), particularly from its role in raising blood pressure.

Liver and Pancreas

Most people are to some extent aware that alcohol can damage the liver, but other than knowing about cirrhosis, which is usually assumed to only affect extreme alcoholics, they do not realise the extent of damage that alcohol can do to the liver. One reason why the liver suffers from drinking too much alcohol is that one of its functions is to remove toxins from the body, and alcohol is a toxin. Over time, the by-products that come about from breaking down these toxins build up in the liver, damaging cells, promoting inflammation and weakening the immune system[15].

Heavy drinking, even over a relatively short period of time, can cause fatty build-up in the liver, which can lead to other illnesses like alcoholic hepatitis. Over more time, this can lead to fibrosis and eventually cirrhosis of the liver. Women are much more susceptible to these conditions, even after relatively moderate drinking. Luckily, the liver is the only organ in the body that has the capacity to regenerate itself, so if you can stop drinking in time and there's not too much damage, your liver will recover---IF you permanently quit drinking.

Alcohol also has severe impacts on the pancreas. What's the pancreas, you may ask, other than the source of the cancer that killed Steve Jobs? It's actually a very important organ, responsible for food digestion, secretion of digestive hormones and of insulin. Alcohol disturbs metabolic processes and damages the pancreas by increasing inflammation. This inflammation is called pancreatitis, and is a leading precursor to pancreatic cancer, which has one of the worst prognoses of common cancers.

Pancreatic disorders also include diabetes; alcohol can both increase and decrease blood sugar which is dangerous for diabetics. Moderate drinking tends to increase blood sugar, increases appetite and potential weight gain, can interfere with diabetes medication and raise triglyceride levels, all of which are potentially hazardous for diabetics. Excessive drinking on the other hand, tends to decrease blood sugar, causing it to drop to dangerous levels, which can be particularly hazardous for Type 1 diabetics.

Cancer

Alcohol increases your risk of contracting a number of different cancers, particularly mouth, esophagus, pharynx, larynx, liver, colon, colorectal and breast cancer. Even a small amount of alcohol can increase the risk of developing certain cancers, and women are more susceptible than men. Smoking significantly increases the cancer risk posed by alcohol.

Recent research seems to indicate that even moderate drinking can raise the risk of metastasis (spread of cancer, which is what actually kills you). Alcohol consumption has been strongly associated with reduced survival rates of various types of cancers, such as oral, pharyngeal, larynx and liver cancer (those cancers which are frequently caused by alcohol)[16]. Recently, alcohol has been linked to increased rates of some types of metastatic breast cancer and also prostate cancer. On the other hand, however, some research has found a negative correlation with metastatic cancer and moderate drinking. This means that *moderate* drinkers can have a reduced risk of metastatic cancer.

Women's Health

Alcohol tends to impact women more than men, often because of its link with hormones such as estrogen and progesterone. In moderation (at recommended limits for women) alcohol can increase blood estrogen, which helps with bone loss after menopause. However, for heavy drinkers, alcohol decreases bone mass, especially in youth, leaving women vulnerable to osteoporosis when they are older[17]. Alcohol also increases the amount of calcium excreted in the urine, further adding to the risk of osteoporosis.

Alcohol's impact on hormones can exacerbate conditions such as Polycystic Ovarian Syndrome (PCOS), fibroids and endometriosis. In the perimenopause period and at premenstrual times, alcohol's impacts on progesterone worsens anxiety and depression. Heavy drinkers may notice that they have 'natural' hot flushes, and drinking in the perimenopause and menopausal period can make these worse, and last longer.

Weight gain

From personal experience, there are two extremely easy ways to lose weight: don't drink alcohol and become a vegetarian/vegan (that is, if you eat properly, not like a friend of mine, who hated vegetables, but went vegan, and lived on potato chips)! This is not a diet book, but I will briefly detail some of the reasons why alcohol makes you put on weight.

Alcohol's impact on weight is quite complex however, but there are a number of ways that it leads to weight gain (and makes it harder to lose weight if you keep drinking). The four ways that alcohol leads to weight gain are:

1. Alcohol is very high in calories, more than carbohydrates and protein, and almost as much as fat. Alcoholic drinks also have other ingredients such as sugars, which can contribute to weight gain (especially premixed drinks).

2. The main contributor to weight gain is not the calories however. Alcohol is processed differently by the liver than other nutrients. As soon as the liver encounters alcohol---which is toxic to the body---it stops burning fat, and burns the alcohol instead. Burning alcohol takes precedence over all other metabolism, and the by-products of this are used for fat storage and energy production[1]. That is why the worst possible thing you can do before or after drinking is to eat calorie dense foods like fried breakfasts and other 'hangover' cures. The calories will go straight to fat. Also, this process can take 24 hours or more, depending on how much you drink, and any exercise or dieting after drinking is a waste of time, as your body is too busy processing the alcohol. If you have drunk a lot, then exercise will probably stress your heart even more, so don't do it.

3. When you drink, you eat more. Alcohol makes you hungry; something which restaurateurs and pub owners are fully aware of, hence the emphasis on serving alcohol with or before food. It is very easy to snack on fatty, salty or sugary foods when drinking.

4. Also, you tend to make more foolish food choices when you drink, eating food that you would otherwise avoid (everyone knows of the 2am kebab or pizza hunger) or mindlessly snacking. Alcohol and mindfulness don't mesh very well.

It's easy to maintain my preferred weight if I don't drink. I don't diet, and I don't stint myself if I want my favourite foods. I generally don't eat junk food (though am partial to twice cooked wedges and corn chips), but when I drink, I eat more, and I tend to weigh about 2kg more than my 'normal' weight.

When I gave up drinking for 5 months, I weighed between 54 and 56kg (depending on my stress levels, I lose weight when I'm stressed). But as soon as I started drinking again, my weight went up to 58/59kg, without any other change in diet, medication or exercise. As soon as I stopped drinking again, my weight stabilised back at 56kg.

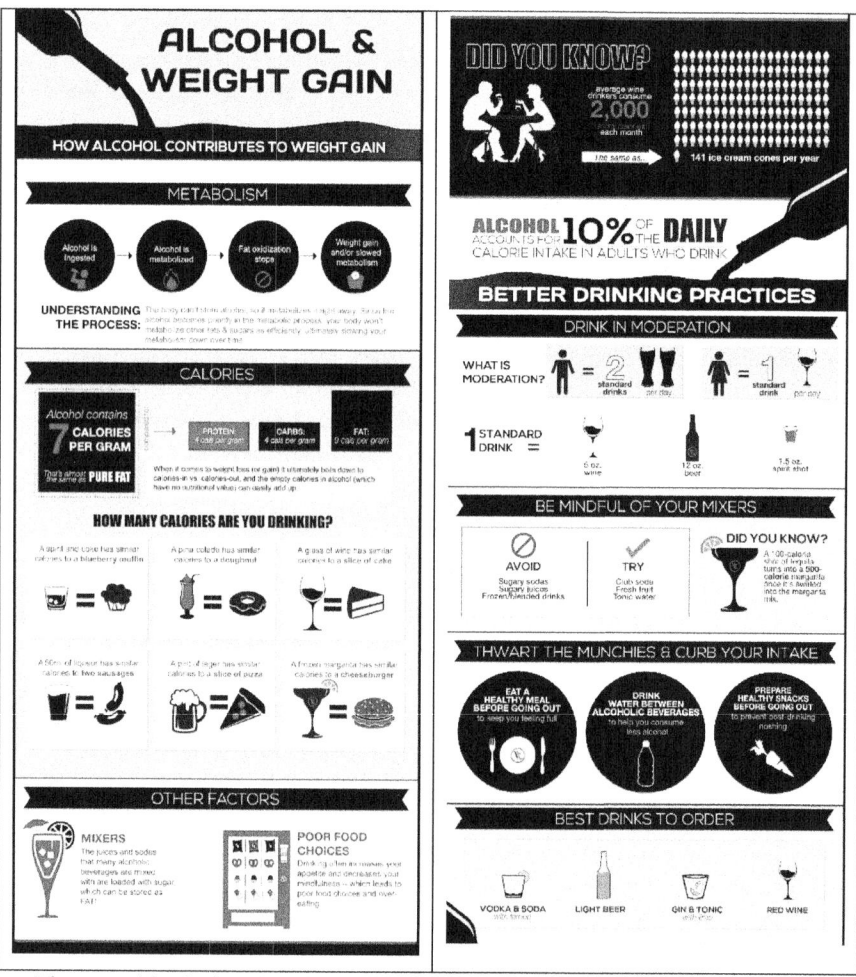

Figure 4 Alcohol and weight gain (source Lucas James[18])

Now, this is a small weight gain and loss, but it is the difference between being comfortable and uncomfortable in my clothes, and the difference between a flabby tummy and a more or less flat one (well, I am 55). I'm not saying that people who have a lot of weight to lose will get rid of it by giving up drinking (for that you might have to become a vegan too, lol) but it will make a difference, and it makes a big difference in maintaining weight.

Other health issues

Drinking alcohol depresses your immune system; leads to weight gain, especially visceral (organ and abdominal) fat; impacts on sleep quality, and has been linked to impacts on the brain (smaller hippocampus in heavy drinkers). Alcohol is bad for the skin, drying it out, and causing blotchiness and burst capillaries. It exacerbates infertility, osteoporosis and chronic kidney disease. Other impacts are to the gut, disturbing the intestinal gut flora, and resulting in poor digestion, diarrhea and other gut problems. Finally, too much alcohol will kill you, either by suffocating on your own vomit, or too much of the poison that is alcohol stopping necessary bodily functions, such as breathing.

Accidents

Alcohol is also implicated in indirect physical harm; it's a leading contributor to accidents, particularly motor vehicle accidents, but also workplace and other accidents, such as falls. Alcohol can also cause harm to others, whether a person under the influence causes a motor vehicle accident injuring or killing others, or a mother drinks too much resulting in a baby with fetal alcohol syndrome.

Another way that alcohol increases the likelihood of physical harm is that many people can show poor judgement if drunk, and may engage in risky sexual behaviour, or do things that put them at risk of sexual assault. When I was younger, for example, I used to do a lot of stupid things whilst drinking, such as hitchhiking, walking alone and late at night in dangerous areas, driving in cars whilst drunk or as a passenger if the driver was drunk, and getting into sexual activities that I would never have done whilst sober.

I was involved in two serious car accidents with drunk drivers; the first conveniently crashed in the entrance of a hospital, and the second could have been fatal. A friend invited me out, but it turned out she was a bit unsure about her new boyfriend, so I was the 'piggy in the middle'. On the way home, he ran out of petrol so borrowed his father's car, which was (fortuitously) a Bentley. I was drunk and not wearing a seatbelt (it was the 80s) and fell asleep in the back. The driver lost control, and the car overturned and skidded across the other side of the highway. I was wearing silky jumpsuit things popular in the 80s, and somehow got a large amount of my buttock skin embedded with bitumen!

After the car had some to a halt, I was trapped in the back. I was terrified, as it was still running and I could smell petrol. I climbed between the headrest and the front seat and got out of the window, and ran for a ditch, where I lay there shivering, waiting for the inevitable Hollywood-type explosion (which didn't happen). When the police came, they had to reassure me that I wasn't going to die in a fiery explosion, and then drive me home. My parents were not amused, particularly as they had to take me to the emergency ward to get the bitumen removed from my bum, which the very unsympathetic emergency ward doctor did without anesthetic, because of my extremely inebriated state.

Subsequently, the father of the guy tried to get me to lie under oath that HE was driving because it turned out that not only was his son drunk, he also didn't have a driver's license! He was only concerned about the fact that his insurance refused to pay for his extremely expensive car, which was totaled. Well, I refused to lie for him. If I had been sober, I would never have gotten into a car with a drunk driver with no license! Well, in retrospect, I wouldn't have---

Sleep

I don't know about you, but I particularly like sleeping, and hate to have disturbed at night (that is why I have banned my cat from the bedroom, as she is prone to waking me up at 3am and demanding food – generally by climbing on to my head and yowling). I have given sleep quality its own heading, as poor sleep quality is one of the major negative effects of alcohol, and can result in other physical and mental problems. For me, getting a good night's sleep is THE major benefit of not drinking---oh, and the fact that it makes it incredibly easy to maintain a healthy weight. Indeed, recent research has indicated that poor sleep quality can lead to weight gain[19], therefore cutting out alcohol can have a double benefit.

Many academic studies have investigated the impacts of alcohol on sleep[20], and the consensus is that the more you drink, the worse your sleep quality. At first, alcohol makes you fall asleep quicker, as it is a sedative (and a depressant) so, for the first part of the night, you sleep deeper. However, once this effect wears off (typically after about 4 hours), you tend to wake up, usually with a raging thirst and headache (if you have drunk too much). Alcohol also seriously impacts on Rapid Eye Movement (REM, not the band, although they named themselves after this) sleep, which is vital for memory, concentration and learning, and also is the stage of sleep in which you dream. It is also the most restorative stage of sleep.

Even a relatively small amount of alcohol is bad for your sleep quality, and women are affected more than men in this regard.

Brain and mental health

Brain health

Alcohol can seriously damage the brain, particularly the developing brain. This is why guidelines are now that pregnant women do not drink any alcohol at all. I know that many of us either drank whilst pregnant, or our parents did, apparently without any ill effects, but really, it is the best for the developing baby to give up alcohol entirely.

Though alcohol does not kill brain cells (as the urban legend says) it is bad for the brain, affecting memory, slowing reaction times and other brain disorders (especially for very heavy drinkers). Alcohol's impacts on the brain depend on a number of factors, such as age when drinking first began and duration of drinking; how much and how often you drink; gender, age, genetics, family history, prenatal exposure to alcohol; and other health issues[21].

Some of the potential effects of drinking on the brain are memory loss, shrinkage of the brain, cognitive changes, and mild to moderate impairment of intellectual capacity.

Alcohol also has multiple indirect impacts on the brain, from the effects of alcohol on other parts of the body, such as the liver, vitamin deficiencies, and the illnesses caused by alcohol. It can also indirectly affect the brain by increasing the likelihood of engaging in risky activities, such as drink driving.

Some types of brain impairment can be reversed through abstinence from alcohol (as can some of the other health impacts, for example, liver damage and mild cardiomyopathy); however, other types of brain damage from alcohol are permanent and irreversible.

Mental health

Alcohol has significant impacts on mental health, contributing to and exacerbating depression and anxiety (amongst others). This is often a two way relationship, as mental health issues can also lead to alcohol abuse, often as a 'quick fix' for feeling bad. But although a drink or more makes you feel better in the short term, in the long term, it is a depressant, and makes you feel worse.

Alcohol also impacts on your brain chemistry, such as levels of serotonin. It is generally accepted that abnormal levels of brain neurotransmitters (chemicals) such as serotonin, are often responsible for many cases of depression, anxiety and obsessive compulsive disorder. This is why a common treatment for such conditions are various types of SSRI[22] (selective serotonin reuptake inhibitor) drugs such as Zoloft, Prozac and Cipramil. These drugs are not without their side effects (both during taking them, and in withdrawal), which can be quite severe, but still, they are effective for many people. On the other hand, if giving up alcohol can achieve similar results, with only positive side effects, then it seems a better choice.

Alcohol is often used to reduce stress, but in the long term, it increases stress. Many chronic drinkers or alcoholics have had significant stress in their lives, particularly in childhood, and frequently report that they began drinking to ease the stress. But alcohol is toxic to the body, and drinking above moderate levels, increases physical stress on organs such as the heart, liver and brain.

Using alcohol as a stress reducer does not teach coping skills or increase resilience and it can raise cortisol levels – thus creating more stress on the body[23][24]. When stressed, cortisol levels rise, increasing heart rate, blood pressure and using more energy for the body to respond. Chronic stress keeps cortisol (and adrenaline, the 'fight or flight' hormone) levels artificially raised, and drinking to reduce stress, in the long term, has the opposite effect.

Interestingly, because alcohol is often used as a Band-Aid solution for extreme stressors, its impact on cortisol levels exacerbates the habitual nature of drinking, as cortisol is linked to habit formation[25].

Excessive alcohol use has also been implicated in other serious mental health problems, such as suicide, self-harm and psychosis. Because alcohol reduces inhibitions, it may trigger a self-harm or suicide attempt, which may not occur when a person is sober. Its role in reducing inhibitions can also result in behaviour that can have long term impacts on mental health, such as placing oneself in danger of sexual and/or violent attacks. In some cases, alcohol can increase violent acts. This is particularly evident when alcohol-fueled riots or large fights take place. These violent acts can cause serious and often long term damage to the mental health both of the perpetrators and the victims, even resulting in Post-Traumatic Stress Disorder (PTSD).

Many serious psychiatric illnesses are either directly caused or exacerbated by alcohol, either used alone or together with illegal drugs such as methamphetamine (ice). Some of these psychiatric disorders include major depression, bipolar disorder and alcoholic/drug-induced psychosis[26]. Luckily, if caught in time, many can be completely reversed by abstinence from alcohol.

I suffer from anxiety, which is mostly expressed in health and social anxiety. My anxiety is reduced while drinking, but as soon as I stop, it comes back worse than before. Alcohol deadens the immediate anxious symptoms, such as obsessive thinking and checking, but it impacts on my sleep quality, so I tend to wake in the middle of the night, and cannot get back to sleep. That is also the time when I have had panic attacks, often because alcohol increases heart rate and palpitations, and there's nothing like 2am palpitations to convince you that you are in imminent danger of a heart attack.

Also, the next morning, you feel terrible, and often do not practice healthy behaviours, such as exercising or meditation, thus negatively impacting on anxiety, so you feel more stressed at work or in response to minor problems. So, you have a drink at night to calm you down, and it becomes a vicious circle.

I am much less anxious if I don't drink. This is rather ironic, as I first started drinking to reduce my social anxiety! But by doing this, I created an alcohol habit, and also engaged in many behaviours that were ultimately detrimental to my physical and mental health. When drinking, I would engage in risky sexual activity, and a couple of times, was sexually assaulted, which at the time, I justified to myself, and buried, but which gave me some long term mental health issues.

If I could give one piece of advice to my younger self, I'd say, "don't drink".

Addiction

As we have seen, alcohol is a toxin, and it is also addictive. I must emphasize that if you are seriously addicted to alcohol, please see a medical professional before trying self-help techniques. This book is aimed more at people for whom drinking a little too much is a habit. However, once you address the addiction aspect of alcohol, with medical help, and 12 step programs such as Alcoholics Anonymous, you can then use the techniques in this book to maintain a no or reduced drinking regime. For some people however, no drinking at all is probably the best way to go. Although I am not addicted to alcohol, for me it is such a strong habit, that if I start drinking again, then I soon revert back to my 2 or 3 glasses of wine a night, so I just don't drink.

FINANCIAL

Alcohol is expensive. Even if you drink cheap wine or beer, the cost adds up. If you are picky about what type of alcohol you drink, it can be very expensive. When I was drinking, I was (well, am) particularly fond of expensive Shiraz from the McLaren Vale area of Australia, and craft beer. At best, a bottle of this wine costs around A$20, and the beers cost around that for a 6-pack. A week's worth of moderate drinking (for me) would be 2 bottles of wine and a 6-pack of beer, which would total around $50 per week. If you add it up, that's around A$2,600 per year, which is about the same as a high season air-ticket to an interesting country. Then, if you add social drinking, wine and beer at a restaurant or pub, you could probably double that (my favourite local craft brewery sells beer at $7.50 per glass).

Giving up or reducing drinking can have significantly positive impacts on your bank balance. What if you put that money, not towards an overseas holiday as I usually do, because I love hiking in Europe, but into your mortgage? If you have an A$400,000 mortgage (more or less the average in Australia---yes, it is a very expensive country for housing), then over 30 years, you pay around double that (another 400k) in interest. If you put an extra $2,600 per year into your mortgage, then you would pay approximately **A$87,000 LESS** (and 5 ½ years less) on your mortgage! Makes you think!

SPIRITUAL

There's good reason why many world faiths prohibit alcohol, either just for their clergy or for everyone. Some religions prohibit it entirely, for example Jainism, Buddhism, Seventh Day Adventists and Islam; and others, such as Judaism, Christianity and Hinduism, allow alcohol in moderation, and as part of ritual and healing, but have strong teachings against drunkenness.

In other spiritual or 'New Age' traditions, alcohol is generally forbidden as it is seen to increase spiritual vulnerability, attract 'black energy' and being an alcoholic (either oneself or a friend or member of the family) is considered as extremely negative. Interestingly, the origin of the word alcohol has been considered to mean 'bad spirit' in Arabic (although there is debate about this, and some scholars link it to the black eyeliner, kohl). Even in English, the word 'spirit' is synonymous with alcohol[27].

In Buddhism, one of the oldest world religions, the teachings of the Buddha were quite clear; alcohol is a poison that clouds the mind. When meditating or practicing mindfulness, alcohol is only a distraction; it gets in the way of concentration, reduces inhibitions and from a purely prosaic perspective, you are likely to fall asleep rather than meditate. Some Buddhists however, do drink alcohol in extreme moderation, taking a few sips, and investigating mindfully its effect on the body and the mind.

The behaviour of a crowd of drunk people is a perfect example of how excessive use of alcohol is the opposite of mindfulness and spirituality. When people drink too much, they might (and frequently do) engage in behaviours that nearly every spiritual tradition would consider 'bad', such as violence and fighting, sexual assault, promiscuity, vandalism, reckless endangerment of themselves and others, and deliberately harming their own bodies by taking in too much poison (alcohol).

From another perspective, the prevalent use of alcohol and its advertising has been seen to be a tool of the global elite to manipulate and control the masses. Why is alcohol is so pervasive throughout our society? Why is it that if you do NOT drink, then you are viewed with suspicion?

Why are major sporting and other events sponsored and promoted by alcohol companies; and that other, far less toxic substances, with spiritual and physical benefits, such as marijuana, are banned?

Whatever your beliefs, if any, alcohol has a long history with spirituality and religion. Speaking only for myself, if I am drinking, I neglect my daily meditation practice (which makes me more anxious), and I find that I am unable to reach deeper levels of attention. If I drink, I also tend to do other more negative actions, such as watching too much TV, eating junk food, and if in a discussion with other people, not listening attentively, and am much more inclined to start an argument and not know when to stop. One of the most important things in any mindfulness or meditation practice, is to learn to pause; when you are drinking, it is much harder to pause.

BUT WHAT ABOUT THE BENEFITS?

Despite all the negatives, alcohol can have many positive benefits, particularly if people drink in moderation. This is a bit of a mixed bag however; it can benefit heart health in moderation, but damage the heart if abused. In moderation, alcohol has been found to:

- "Reduce your risk of developing and dying from heart disease
- Possibly reduce your risk of ischemic stroke (when arteries to your brain become narrowed or blocked, causing reduced blood flow)
- Possibly reduce your risk of diabetes"[1]

As is increasingly the case however, research shows that only *some* people benefit from moderate drinking, and others can tolerate very little, if any, alcohol. Indeed, counter to popular belief, only about 15% of people have the specific gene that gives them benefits from drinking[28]. So moderate drinking only benefits quite a small number of people.

Other people, such as those from some eastern Asian countries, have a gene that makes them very susceptible to the effects of alcohol, causing facial flushing, headaches and nausea, even after consuming only a small amount of alcohol. For this reason, and other socio-cultural reasons (such as alcohol not being a customary part of some societies) these countries have lower levels of alcoholism than countries where alcohol is an intrinsic part of the culture.

In Western countries, a problem is that many people think that their alcohol consumption is moderate, when in fact, it is quite heavy. For example, it is recommended that women drink no more than 200ml of wine (a smallish wine glass) a day; whereas many people may drink two or more glasses, particularly over a long period of time.

Counter arguments will highlight that there are very high levels of drinking in places such as France, Italy and Spain, yet people in these countries have relatively low levels of heart disease. Perhaps with a degree of wishful thinking, the assumption is then that these benefits are solely due to the consumption of wine. However, it is not accurate to look at one variable apart from other potentially confounding variables. Yes, people in these countries **do** drink a lot of wine, but they also drink wine as part of a meal, slowly, and together with other heart friendly activities such as more exercise, lower stress levels and fresh, locally sourced food. Moreover, there are very high levels of drinking in Europe, especially in some northern and eastern countries, where they tend to binge drink rather than drink in moderation every day as they tend to do in Italy and France.

It also depends on what you drink. I know many people who have their one glass of whiskey, or even wine, a day, and are quite happy doing so. I personally can drink no more than 2 beers, unless I am really thirsty, so have no problem drinking beer in moderation. However, for me, wine is my nemesis. I love wine, and find that restricting this to only one glass is almost impossible (not that I ever really enjoy the second and third glasses mind you). So for me, and believe me, I have tried, I am better off not drinking wine at all. And as the only other alcoholic drink I like is beer, so I just drink non-alcoholic beer, as it tastes largely the same (to me) as ordinary beer. (Yes, I am probably a beer Philistine, but I am way too old to care about fashion or fads---I also prefer instant coffee!)

Substitutes for Alcohol

However, substituting soft drinks for alcohol is no better. Soft drinks are just empty calories, full of sugar and preservatives; and the diet ones are even worse, with the sugar substitutes playing havoc with your insulin levels (conversely, making you hungrier).

I don't like sweet drinks myself, which is why I find beer such a refreshing drink. As mentioned above, I am quite happy to drink non-alcoholic beer. Indeed, I wish that pubs and restaurants would serve this, as it tastes like 'real' beer, and saves social pressure on you to drink. Otherwise, in a pub or similar setting, I will drink soda or tonic water, lemon lime and bitters (though I find this too sweet) or ginger beer (ditto). Be careful that you don't get alcoholic ginger beer (which is very nice by the way).

At home I drink sparkling grape juice (or still grape juice if I can find it), herbal teas, coffee, soda water, and kombucha. I love kombucha, and it is very good for you because it is probiotic (incidentally, if you DO 'inadvertently' drink too much, it is excellent for hangovers!)

You can also Google non-alcoholic drinks, such as mocktails, smoothies, herbal drinks, etc. Some of these are wonderful, and taste way nicer than alcohol. I have a favourite, which is soda water, sparkling grape juice (or non-alcoholic sparkling wine), strawberries, ice and mint. Gorgeous. Soda water, mint and lemon or lime is also lovely. In winter, various herbal teas, hot chocolate or Milo are great warming drinks

Dealing with social pressure

This is one of the worst aspects of giving up drinking, especially if your friends know you as the life of the party or the one they always tag in Facebook posts about wine. Some people will welcome you giving up drinking, but others, perhaps feeling guilty about their own drinking, will subtly (and not so subtly) try and persuade you to drink. They will say things like, 'it's not as if you are an alcoholic' or 'wine is good for you' or 'just one won't harm you'. Another problem is, that if everyone is drinking and you are not, then their behaviour can rapidly become quite irritating!

There are various strategies you can use to deal with this. You can drink non-alcoholic drinks and not make a point of the fact that you aren't drinking (most people won't notice, especially if they are having a few themselves). You can also volunteer to be the designated driver. In my experience, this is always welcomed. There is a drawback to this however, in that your friends often think that they can drink as much as they like, and the drunker they get, the less appealing they are to the newly sober you. My tolerance for staying out late, especially if everyone else is drunk, is very limited, so I stay home.

If you are very assertive, you can just say no, I don't drink anymore and don't explain anything. If you are less assertive, you can make up some excuse, like Dry July, FebFast, side effects of medication, or an allergy. I've found the latter not to work sometimes, as people will try and foist their favourite organic wine (or whatever) on you instead. My favourite excuse is allergies, and if pressed, I tell them that wine gives me diarrhea! They normally back off quickly, in case I am inclined to elaborate on this. Younger women can say they are trying to get pregnant, and if they are pregnant, they should avoid drinking.

A fantastic excuse (and true) for not drinking might be that you are on diet (almost everyone is always on some diet or other). As explained above, If you drink too much, you tend to put on weight more easily (see above), and if you are dieting, then you shouldn't be drinking.

If you are organising social occasions in your home or elsewhere (not in a pub or restaurant), you can organise day time activities, such as rock climbing or kayaking or hiking. None of these activities go very well with alcohol---and if you are considering combining rock climbing with drinking, I would strongly suggest against it! Or you could meet for coffee in the morning instead of evening activities. I prefer this type of socialising, so it is easy for me to organise and attend such events and I don't like driving at night anyway.

Sometimes, until your friends get used to you not drinking, you might just have to not socialise with the same people. Sadly, some people lose their friends by not drinking, because their friends are so enmeshed in the drinking culture that they **cannot** socialise with people who don't drink. In that case, you might want to find some new friends, who are more similar to you and more in tune with your new lifestyle and values.

CHAPTER 3: THE SCIENCE OF HABIT AND BEHAVIOUR CHANGE

"Nature never appeals to intelligence until habit and instinct are useless"
H. G. Wells

THE PHYSIOLOGICAL BASIS OF HABIT FORMATION

As we saw in the previous chapter, alcohol can have many, often negative, physiological effects on the body, including physical and psychological addiction.

To emphasize again, if you have a serious problem with alcohol, please see a medical professional first. This book is not aimed at people with serious medical issues.

Nonetheless, even if you are physically addicted to alcohol; cutting down or giving it up also requires addressing the **HABIT** of drinking. Of course, this can apply to **any** habit that you wish to modify, so although the focus of this book is on alcohol, the information and techniques can also be applied to other habits, such as smoking or binge eating.

The word 'habit' can be defined as:

> - "a behaviour pattern acquired by frequent repetition or physiologic exposure that shows itself in regularity or increased facility of performance,
> - an acquired mode of behaviour that has become nearly or completely involuntary, or
> - addiction"

There are two types of habit formation; physiological and psychological[29]. This chapter describes the physiological basis and the following chapter describes the psychological/behavioural basis of habit formation.

To fully understand how habits are formed and how they persist, we first need to understand some of the neuroscience behind habit formation. After all, no matter what we do, our behaviour originates in our nervous system, and in our brain. How our bodies and minds work are what determine how we behave.

Of course, if you are not interested in learning about the basis of habit formation, then you can of course, just skip to the chapters about the technique, or look up funny cat videos on YouTube, but I think that it is both useful and interesting to know *why*

HUMAN INSTINCT AND HOW THE BRAIN CREATES HABITS

Many animals operate on instinct. Instinct is automatic behaviour; that is, neither learned nor controlled by the conscious mind. For example, the pathetically small pink bean that is a baby kangaroo instinctively moves towards the mother's pouch; or birds instinctively know that a snake is dangerous, even if they have never seen one before. All animals display some form of instinct, but the higher the animal (in terms of intellect), the less likely that behaviour is instinctive, and the more likely it's a result of some sort of learning, even of consciousness. In the past, however, psychologists attributed many *human* behaviours to instinct, but this concept has largely fallen out of favour.

Regardless, humans do exhibit another type of behaviour, which is very often unconscious---and this is termed **habitual behaviour.**

Just like motor cars, computers and coral reefs, humans are what is known as a system. Systems are sets of interdependent, interacting, related components. Systems are characterised by structure, behaviour, interconnectivity and communication.

So why are systems important to understand behaviour? Bear with me, while I give a very simple explanation of how the human brain and the nervous and endocrine systems control our behaviour.

Ok, say you are driving down the highway, and all of a sudden, white smoke pours from under the hood, your car loses power and comes to a juddering halt. Now, assume that you have managed to avoid being rear-ended by the enormous truck that's been tailgating you for the last 10km, and that you have managed to safely pull off the road, where you are more or less out of imminent danger of being ridden over by some moron updating his Facebook profile or taking a selfie in the rear view mirror. What do you do?

BREAKING THE BOOZE HABIT

If you know anything about how a car system works, you might immediately (and carefully) lift the hood and check if the radiator has overheated. Although, if you know anything about cars, you probably would have noticed that the car's temperature had started to rise long before this happened. However, if you are anything like me, you will have either not noticed, or ignored it, in the hope that it would go away on its own. Unlike what usually happens when you take your car to the mechanic and the problem immediately disappears (until you drive away), this sort of problem usually gets worse.

So you stop the car, lift the hood, and stare perplexedly into the engine. I usually prod a couple of things or jiggle a few wires to see if they are loose, pretending that I know what I'm doing. Of course, I have utterly no idea what anything in an engine is or what it does, except for the oil filler bit and the windscreen wiper water replacement tank (and even then I usually have to sneakily consult the manual), and it's usually all dirty, and I don't like touching grease. I even once had to consult the manual on how to fill up my fuel tank---the problem is, I was at the truck filling bowser at the service station; so there I am, standing there, reading the manual, surrounded by enormous tattooed truckies with ZZ Top beards and singlets barely covering their vast beer kegs; and the fuel came out at such a pace, that it overflowed and spilled all over my car and my feet. Suffice it to say, the truckies thought it was hilarious. In my defense, I had just moved from a country where there is driveway service, and I had never had to fill up a fuel tank before. Oh first world problems!

In the case of the overheating car, and assuming that I have forgotten to update my RACQ membership, I then stand on the side of the road and look pathetic, and wait for some kind, mechanically minded soul to come and help me (and hope they are not going to cart me off into the bushes and molest me instead of helping a damsel in distress—note, yes, I know, am about the furthest from a damsel that you can imagine)

Generally speaking, this worked a lot better at 23 than at 55, which is why I have a RACQ membership (um, it's lapsed, but I had one). It's remarkably simple to stand on the side of a road and look pathetic when you are an attractive 20-something old. No wonder I never learned anything about cars. Nevertheless, an overheating radiator is a simple thing to remedy, at least until you can get the car to the service station. Therefore, if you can understand how one thingy is attached to another thingy and what third thingy it moves; then you can (sort of) understand the system---and then you can change things.

Therefore in the context of the human system, if you can understand how the things work together, you can understand how to fix them, or at least to make them work better. But of course, you might say, and quite correctly; humans are not cars (although some little boys think they are).

However, we *are* systems, but incredibly complex systems, unlike the rather simplistic internal combustion engine (which is only simple in comparison to a human). In fact human behaviour is the result of a multitude of complex sub systems, all working together to create a highly functioning whole.

In a human being like you or I, two major systems contribute to our behaviour. These are the nervous system (the brain, spinal cord, nerves etc.) and the endocrinal system (hormonal influences). The brain is the control center of the body, and it's made up of a vast and complicated network of neurons, or nerve cells. A normal adult brain performs approximately 100 trillion calculations a second. You may disagree, if stranded on the side of the road and desperately trying to avoid the twits driving and talking and texting on their mobile phones, who surely only share a single brain cell between them, and it's not functioning in any other way than an apparent desire to win a Darwin Award[30]. Nevertheless, it's true. And incidentally, the idea that humans only use 10% of their brains is sadly, a myth, and there's no way we can gain super powers by utilising the other 90%.

The nervous system is made up of the **Peripheral Nervous System (PNS)** and the **Central Nervous System (CNS)**. The **PNS** comprises the nerves that radiate around the body, communicating sensations of what you feel to the brain. If you are clumsy like I am, and you frequently cut yourself as I do, then that horrible feeling of the knife entering your flesh is your nerves signaling their discomfort to the brain. Gives me the heebs just thinking about it.

The **PNS** is differentiated into the somatic nervous system (which transmits sensations like the rather unpleasant feel of the stick I stood on yesterday, as it entered my flesh; and it is also responsible for voluntary movement and action) and the automatic nervous system. The automatic nervous system is responsible for involuntary but quite important things like breathing, heartbeat and digestion. It's also responsible for emotional responses like crying and laughter, and the instinctive pulling away or the screech of pain, for example, when you stand on a sharp stick or whack your shin with a mattock.

The **CNS** is the brain and the spinal cord. The 'building blocks' of the CNS are the neurons, or nerves. Neurons form most of the brain and spinal cord. The CNS is essential to human functioning, so the spinal column and brain are protected by thick bones like the skull and spine, as well as muscles and other inside stuff.

Inside the brain, the hypothalamus gland connects the endocrine and nervous system. The endocrine system is not related to the nervous system, but is vital to communication. The endocrine system is comprised of glands around the body, which produce chemicals called hormones, which are then sent to various areas of the body, and perform a multitude of different functions.

The endocrine system is very much more complex than the popular concepts of hormones, but like all myths, there is a grain of truth in these stereotypes. Hormones are responsible for a vast array of different behaviours. They can trigger new behaviours, or modify existing behaviours. They can also assist in responding to future situations; for example the 'love' hormone Oxytocin[31] not only makes you feel good, but can strengthen social memory in certain parts of the brain. For example, if you were bullied at school, as I was, the brain uses these memories to anticipate the same thing happening in the future, leading to fear and anxiety in certain situations, such as when gangs of teenage girls (also known as hockey teams) come running at you, brandishing lethal weapons (aka hockey sticks).

Why the brain likes to form habits (it needs LOTS of energy)

The various systems of the body, including the CNS, use a LOT of energy. Many of us think that the major use of energy comes from the physical activity that we (hopefully) do every day, but this is not true. The body part that uses the most energy is the brain[32]. Energy use by the brain (or CNS) comprises 20% of our basal metabolic rate (see box).

Now, although the brain needs so much energy, it's quite 'lazy' and doesn't like to expend energy on unnecessary things, like the same behaviour that is practiced often and in the same way. Therefore, our brain is just like us (well, it *is* us). If we can sit on the couch and a particularly irritating advertisement comes on TV, and changing it merely entails clicking the remote control to change the channel, then we will happily click away---but if we have to physically get up to change the channel, I bet most of us will just grin and bear it---whilst of course, having a whinge.

Well, thinking is also hard work---if you don't believe me, try doing some complicated mathematical or logic puzzles or studying for an important exam---and the brain has a lot of other functions to worry about, such as keeping the heart beating, or monitoring the chemical balance of the body (the more important stuff, that luckily, we don't have to think about, otherwise some of us would probably forget to breathe, or to maintain the optimal glucose balance of our blood---whatever that might be).

You can liken the brain to the CEO of a multinational company. Does the CEO bother him or herself with every tiny detail, such as the weekly processing of the pay of all employees or what is served in the canteen in a regional office? Of course not---unless s/he happens to eat there on a field trip and the food is awful, or if they are a micromanager. S/he has minions to do that.

Energy use in the body

There are three major ways in which your brain uses calories: the basal metabolic rate, physical activity and the thermic effect of food[1].

First, the basal metabolic rate (BMR) is how much energy your body needs to function at rest (sitting, sleeping, even watching TV). The BMR also includes the energy needed for things like keeping your heart beating, lungs working, and all the other stuff that happens inside your body that pretty much keeps you alive and breathing. The BMR comprises 60-70% of all energy used by the body (depending on how active you are, because the more muscle you have, the higher your BMR). People living in very cold climates also need more food, as keeping the body temperature at an even level in places such as the Arctic, requires a higher intake of calories. That's why polar explorers can eat such huge meals and not get fat. They have really cool hipster beards too; which men find it easier to grow than most women.

Second is physical activity, or how much energy you need to fuel any physical activity. For some, such as professional athletes, this may include intense exercise every day, and for others, such as 'couch potatoes', it might include walking to your car, or to the refrigerator. Obviously an athlete needs to take in a lot more energy (i.e. food) than a couch potato, although often the latter may eat more total calories, but not burn it off.

Finally, the thermic effect of food is the amount of energy expended in eating and digesting the food, which sadly, is only about 10%. Thus, if you eat 500 calories of food, this will use up 10% of the calories, making it equivalent to 50 calories or about half an apple.

So, as you can see, most of our energy used is by the BMR, which is why this is so often used in weight loss calculations. Here is a good calculator that will tell you approximately how many calories you need per day just to survive (http://www.bmi-calculator.net/bmr-calculator/). Because I'm quite small and slim, and in my 50s, my BMR was only 1236 calories, which isn't very much. But that means my brain uses at least a fifth of that (I wonder if working as an academic means that my brain uses more energy)? However, I'm sorry to tell most of you, that thinking hard is not going to burn more calories, so you aren't going to lose any weight that way.

Our brains are similar. If the brain can make something into a habit, which it doesn't have to think about, it will do so. This is one reason why habits are so hard to break. The brain doesn't like extra work, and resists it with great effort. Yep, our brains are indeed just like us. The box below has a semi scientific explanation of the brain's energy use[33].

> **What the brain uses energy for**
>
> Two thirds of the brain's energy use is to help neurons (nerve cells) fire (electrical impulses that pass between neurons to communicate with one another).
>
> The remaining third of the brain's energy is used for what some scientists call 'housekeeping', which includes keeping cells healthy, and maintaining the ionic balance of nerve cells, so that they can fire effectively.
>
> The primary source of this cellular energy is a chemical by the name of adenosine triphosphate (ATP)
>
> To function effectively, cells need to maintain something called ionic (or hydrogen ion) balance, which means keeping ions (or chemicals, such as sodium and chloride) in balance on either side of a cell membrane
>
> ATP supplies the energy for these ions to go through cell membranes.

Ok, now we know that the brain takes up 20% of the energy use of the body, but that it is lazy and doesn't like to expend this energy on doing stuff that's repeated every day. Aren't facts wonderful? If you ever get asked this in a trivia competition, you will have at least one question correct. But how does this relate to habits, and to behaviour?

Rewiring the brain, or, are habits just instinct?

Everything we do and think originates in the brain, and this is dictated by electrical impulses in the neurons and chemicals transmitting back and forth.

When any behaviour is repeated often enough, the pathways in the brain to perform that behaviour get used to this, with the result that, in future, it is easier for the electrical impulses to travel that path. The behaviour thus becomes habitual[34]. To quote Donald Hebb, '*neurons that fire together wire together*'[35].

So what does that mean? A good analogy might be to look at a suburban yard, say a house down the street where I last lived. The owners of the house had a fenced garden, with a wire mesh fence, and a large Dalmatian, Spot. When the owners go to work, they leave Spot outside in the yard.

Spot is bored, so every time another dog goes past, he can see it through the fence, and charges up and down frantically barking and growling, guarding his territory, or just being plain mean. Over time, Spot wears a deep rut in the lawn, where the grass doesn't grow. Because Spot does this a lot, it is easier for him to run in the same rut along the fence.

This is a simplistic analogy of what happens when a habit is formed; a 'rut' (or thicker area of neurons) forms in the verdant lawn of your brain. Well, *my* brain is less like a verdant lawn and more like a field with weeds of a thousand different species, but you get the picture.

> **You are not very observant---selective attention**
>
> Fascinatingly, we actually observe very little of our day to day world (one reason why eyewitness testimony is not given serious credence in many contemporary court cases).
>
> In a famous psychological experiment, groups of students were told to watch a video of two teams (one dressed in black and the other in white) and asked to count how many times the players dressed in white passed the ball.
>
> However, in the middle of the game, a person dressed in a black gorilla suit walked across the screen, stopped in the middle, beat their chest and walked off again.
>
> You would think that everyone would notice something so obvious, wouldn't you?
>
> Well, up to 80% of people DIDN'T notice.
>
> The brain is very good at paying selective attention to the world around it, and if distracted by something (like being asked to count how many times a ball is passed) it is very good at not noticing much else around it---even something as odd as a person in a gorilla suit.

Therefore, actions that you perform every day often become habitual, or instinctive. You don't *think* about cleaning your teeth, or driving your car, or anything like that; these actions have become habits. But remember when you were learning to drive, or to play a horrendously complicated sport like golf. It wasn't that easy then (well, golf is never easy, no matter how much you practice), and you had to actively think about every single step you took. It was really difficult to move the stick shift at the same time as move the steering wheel, and also look out for other cars, seemingly hell-bent on killing you. But one day, you just got in your car, and drove, and realised, after some time, that you had done it all without thinking. Driving had become a habit. This is known as 'procedural memory'[36].

It's also a reason why we are often quite oblivious of the world around us. We are actually terribly unobservant, and rather bad at remembering things. We pay only selective attention to stuff around us---even people in gorilla suits!

Now for the really technical stuff. Habit forming is not quite as simple as I have just described, and there are many parts of the brain that are involved in the process. These include the anterior cingulate cortex, orbitofrontal cortex and dorsolateral prefrontal cortex (I'm glad I'm not a medical student having to write a closed book exam on this; social science is much easier).

Anterior cingulate cortex

The Anterior Cingulate Cortex (ACC) is a part of the brain that sits below the main cortex, and is also known as Brodmann Area 25 (wonder if it has UFOs----oh wait, that's Area 51). It also has the most well connected neurons in the brain[37]. It's known for a type of neuron called the Von Economo Neuron (sounds like a Bond villain, 'let's go and search Baron Von Economo Neuron's secret lair'), and these neurons are extensively interconnected with other neurons in the brain, and also more abundant in humans than other species; although primates also have these cells.

The ACC is associated with empathy, creativity, meditation and risk assessment; it links with the nerves in the gut, and most importantly, in the context of this book, with reward-related tasks. It's also highly important to the maintenance of motivation by its function in mood regulation, the reassessment of values and goals, and learning how to delink habits from triggers. This is also known as the associative theory of habit formation.

But wait, what does this *mean*? Basically, this means that a habit can form in certain situations, by repeating the same action---such as having a drink when you get home, or a cigarette after a meal---and after a time, the habit persists, even if the trigger (coming home, or eating) does not occur. This is also relevant to breaking habits. It also means that both good and bad habits are often formed because of rewards.

Rewards, by the way, are not just *physical*, like money, but can be much more ephemeral, including feeling good about doing (or not doing) something. These **intangible rewards** are often much stronger than purely physical or financial rewards.

Orbitofrontal cortex (also known as Striatum)

The orbitofrontal cortex (OFC) is found just behind the eyes. It's a relatively poorly understood area of the brain, but researchers theorise that it's involved in cognitive decision-making, expectation, adaptive learning and the affective value of reinforcers. The OFC is subdivided into three subregions, one of which "*...codes the subjective experience of pleasure such as food and sex*"; one which "*...monitors the valence, learning, and memory of reward values*" and the last is active when "*...when punishers force a behavioral change*"[38].

The OFC therefore appears relevant to alerting the brain to rewards and punishments of an action, based on cues in a particular situation[39]. In particular, rewards, expected rewards and even the subjective and sensory appeal of reinforcers (such as the first taste of a good wine) are located in the OFC. This is important in the context of habit, as the sensory appeal (how pleasant it is) of drinking alcohol is not the same as thirst or the desire for a drink[40], and for many of us, our drinking habits are excellent examples of this. The box below shows how another type of habit, eating junk food, is manipulated by manufacturers to deliberately create artificial desires for their products. Alcohol is similar, and advertisers will use images such as an attractive, successful looking couple having a drink on an expensive yacht, whilst watching a beautiful sunset; thus associating drinking with relaxation, romance, affluence and social status; aspirational goals for many.

Further supporting this concept is that the OFC is involved in addictive, compulsive and repetitive behaviour. Functional MRI has shown that this part of the brain is linked to the activation of reward circuits, and is particularly marked in people who are dependent on certain addictive drugs. In addition, this part of the brain is also linked with compulsive gambling; those with OFC dysfunction are less able to stop gambling once they have started.

Interestingly, people with Obsessive Compulsive Disorder (OCD) often have an overactive OFC[41] Functional MRI and PET scans of people with OCD have shown increased activity in the OFC, as well as imbalances of neurotransmitters dopamine and serotonin. The compulsive actions displayed by many who suffer from OCD are essentially "*...manifestations of excessive habit formation*"[42]. It is hypothesized that people with OCD are not displaying goal-directed behaviour, rather that the compulsions are very strong habits that are highly resistant to any conscious desire to change or eliminate them[43].

The OFC is therefore integral to habit formation, which are often a learned response to a situation in a stable context. The OFC triggers sensory feelings in response to a reinforcer or cue, such as alcohol, junk food or cigarettes. In combination with the physically addictive characteristics of some of these, such as alcohol, this can make giving up our favourite addictions very difficult.

Junk food and why people crave it

The junk food industry is huge and extremely lucrative. Food scientists spend fortunes on formulating the exact combination of sugar, fat and salt to keep us coming back for more (as this keeps the shareholders happy, and the CEO's private jets maintained to his exacting standards). For example, let's say that someone has a habit of eating crisps, say, Grain Waves or Doritos (ok, I 'fess up). When faced with a large packet of Grain Waves, a person might start eating, and not stop until the whole packet is finished and they end up flattening out the packet and licking the tiny crumbs off the bottom (haven't done this before have we?) Junk foods such as this are specifically manufactured to have sensory appeal, the crunchiness of the chip itself, the salty flavour, the combination of artificial chemical flavourants and so on.

Food manufacturers spend millions of dollars just on getting the exact degree of crunch in chips or the fizz in a soft drink[1]. Their scientists concentrate on a number of factors to keep customers coming back for more and more, and to prevent the brain from becoming bored, and looking for new sources of stimulation. Some of these include:

- *Rapid meltdown. Foods that rapidly dissolve once you begin chewing, but are also high in calories (potato chips, chocolate) are more appealing, and much 'moreish'.*
- *Sensory specific response. The brain gets bored quite rapidly with similar foods (try one of those fad diets where you just eat a small range of foods to see what I mean). However, junk food is specifically designed to provide enough variety and taste to be interesting, which is why you can eat a whole packet of chips and not a whole cabbage---and you fart less too.*
- *Calorie density. Many junk foods are high in calories, but relatively low in fiber. This means that you can eat a lot of them before you feel full. Try eating a cup of dry sugar-frosted flakes or a cup of dry Weetabix to see what I mean (and ditto my previous comment about gas).*
- *Memories of past easting experiences. This is where the OFC really comes into play, and which is directly related to why you may have a junk food habit. When you eat something really tasty (like GrainWaves or Doritos) your brain remembers that feeling. When you even think about that food, it causes the brain to trigger the memories of the sensations of easting that food, and even cause you to salivate, just by thinking about the food---that is, just before you get up and go down to the shop or vending machine to buy some. Noooo, you have work to do*

Dorsolateral prefrontal cortex

The dorsolateral prefrontal cortex (DLPFC) is one of the most advanced parts of the brain, and continues to develop well into adulthood[44]. It's found at the top of the prefrontal cortex, just about where the top of your forehead and hairline begins (that is, if you are not bald, or like me, are growing out a really bad haircut). It has a range of functions, and those which are of relevance to habits include its functions of cognitive processing, decision making, memory and planning.

Obviously, this part of the brain is directly related to your realisation and cognitive evaluation that a given habit is something you wish to create, modify or eliminate entirely. Once you have done so, then it's involved in the decision to get rid of or reduce the habit (or on the other side, it can also be used to create a new positive habit, such as eating more fruit and vegetables or engaging in regular exercise). And of course, its planning function helps you research tactics to break the habit (including buying books such as this), starting a habit diary, writing on a calendar, monitoring the behaviour, and planning situations that will not expose you to the cues that usually trigger the habit.

Amygdala

The amygdala is involved in the processing and memory of emotion, and is also linked to the intensity of flavour of a food or drink and the desire to eat or drink more[45,46]. Also, the amygdala is the region of the brain that is most strongly liked to emotions and stress, and because of this, researchers think it's also strongly linked to addiction and habit.

We frequently learn to associate emotions with positive or negative events, places, or things. Some scientists think that this (apart from genetic differences) is one of the reasons why people become anxious. Anxiety is of course, part of human nature, and important to our survival. If past humans were not anxious and alert to potential threats in the surrounding environment, say an ominous rustle in the undergrowth, or a large, funnel shaped cloud; then they likely would not have survived to create more humans. However, for anxious people, our natural wariness has become over sensitive, so we are now anxious about things which are not really threatening or pose any danger to us, such as imaginary illnesses or having to speak in public.

For example, as a child, I enjoyed regular trips to a coastal town on my school holidays. When I return to that town, or even when I just think about it or the ocean, the memory brings about pleasant emotions based on my childhood memories. I remember little about the actual town (and am sure that most of which I remember is wrong) but the emotions are as strong as ever.

On the other hand, unpleasant experiences can bring about unpleasant emotions. When I was going through a bad breakup, my then partner (who was overseas) used to phone me on Skype. Every time he rang, we would end up having a huge fight. Now, just hearing the sound of the Skype ringtone can trigger a whole gamut of horrible emotions, such as a sinking feeling of dread and anxiety, and also physical symptoms, such as a racing heartbeat and nausea.

The aspect of amygdala function that is most relevant to habit formation, is something called cue anticipation, which are the environmental cues which can trigger the performance of the habitual action, including addictive behaviour. Because of the amygdala's role in emotional memory, it forms associations between the pleasant nature of the experience (say, for a drinker, the taste of your first beer) and the cues that give rise to that experience (which might be getting home after a day at work, getting the beer out of the fridge, and taking the first deep mouthful).

The more that the person performs the same actions in the same situation, the more likely it's that the brain will form an association between the action, the response, and the cues, thus creating a habit. This persists long after the pleasant nature of the habit has disappeared (for example, in smoking, which rapidly becomes quite unpleasant).

However, using cues is an excellent method to break a habit too; you can also create an 'easy' or 'good' habit as a cue to breaking a 'bad' habit. For example, you could get into the habit of weighing yourself every morning at the same time, or writing how many drinks you had the night before, and then writing these figures down on a visible place, like a calendar.

Once you have set up this simple habit, say writing your drinks had on a calendar every morning, you can use this as a trigger to set up a habit to stop or cut down your drinking.

Ok, so now we (sort of) understand the brain functions behind habit formation. But what about the behavioural aspects of habit formation?

CHAPTER 4 THE PSYCHOLOGICAL BASIS OF HABIT FORMATION

"We become what we repeatedly do"
Sean Covey

INTRODUCTION

As we saw in the previous chapter, habits have a physiological origin in the brain; in how neural pathways are formed and strengthened, in how the brain likes to conserve its energy for important stuff (like keeping us alive) and in how various parts of the brain are involved in habit formation.

Habits are, obviously, neither good nor bad. We may think certain things are 'bad' and they may well be for us, but habit forming is an important part of human behaviour. We'd be exhausted if we had to constantly *think* about habitual things, like cleaning our teeth or driving our cars (although, some people probably *should* think more when driving).

Just as in the old 'nature vs nurture' debate (where philosophers argue whether our characters are based on our genetics or our environment), habits also have a psychological basis, and influence and even control our behaviour in everyday life. Because after all, our habits are ultimately an everyday, common occurrence---otherwise, they wouldn't be habits.

Associative vs Script-Based

There are two major schools of thought as to the overarching behavioural mechanisms of habit formation; the associative and the script-based theory[1].

In the **associative model** of habit formation, a learned association forms between stimulus (the thing which incites to action, for example, a certain time of day or a certain location), and response (the action which is carried out, for example, having a drink).

BREAKING THE BOOZE HABIT

If the behaviour is carried out often enough in the same context, then an association is formed in the brain, and a new neural pathway is established (for example, the neighbours get a new puppy so your dog decides to run along the back fence instead of the front fence, thus creating a new rut).

After this neural pathway becomes stronger, it takes precedence over other neural pathways (grass---or more likely, weeds---then grow over the old rut), and it's no longer necessary to think or make any elaborate decisions about the behaviour, it has, in other words, become habitual.

Say that Mary starts a new job, which is relatively stressful. A couple of days a week, on returning home, she goes outside to her deck and has a glass of wine. The action of sitting down for half an hour, as well as the depressive effect on the central nervous system of the wine, serves to relax Mary.

After a while, she started to do this *every day* at 5.30pm, and before long, she no longer thinks about the actions involved in having her glass of wine, but sometimes, without even thinking about it, finds herself sitting on her deck, drinking wine. She also looks forward to this little ritual, does it weekends too.

The associative approach to habit formation assumes for some actions, the resulting behaviour is either habitual or deliberate, but not both. The associative approach forms learned associations between goals and motivations.

The pertinent point is that **behaviours become linked through repeated practicing in stable contexts**, leading to an association of the behaviour with that **context**, or **cues** around that context.

Thus, Mary's habitual wine drinking may not be associated directly with sitting on her deck, but rather to the context of coming home after work, and/or the relaxed feeling that she gets after the first few sips.

The other theory of habit formation is the **script-based theory** of habit formation. A cognitive script is a type of rule that says, in a certain situation, a specific type of behaviour is adequate[1]. This sounds complicated, but think about people who work in a call center. They all have scripts from which they work, with various choices according to what the caller says. These scripts are used in all types of situations, including in emergency services.

Well, this is basically what we do when forming habits. We have an internal script that tells us that when situation A occurs, we then perform behaviour B. Of course it is much more complex than this, but basically the scripts result in the same benefit to the brain---less use of thinking energy required when performing regular behaviours.

---

[1] Probably not relevant to perfectionists, lol

Just imagine that every time someone called 000 (or 911), the call center operator had to go into Dr Google or WebMD and research every possible scenario. It would take forever, and many more people would die. Instead they ask questions like, 'do you need police, ambulance or fire'? And, 'is he breathing', 'is he bleeding', 'do you know what type of snake bit him'? They usually avoid asking some questions, which would require unnecessarily complex (and often bizarre) explanations, such as 'what was he doing to the crocodile before it attacked him'[47] or 'why was he cleaning his roof at 2am'2? In this way, the script enables the operator to rapidly provide the correct information, and (hopefully) dispatch immediate help.

Of course, scripts go wrong, and there are many situations where a decision tree type script will not suffice, but we are talking about habits, which are common, everyday occurrences. When the zombie apocalypse hits, it's everyone to their own---unless you know Daryl Dixon and you remember that whilst a tiny scratch will inevitably cause you to shuffle around, plaintively pleading for 'brains, brains, brains', you can be covered from head to toe with zombie blood and remain unscathed.

Repetition, Automaticity and Stability

Breaking down the associative or script based mechanisms, we can see that some fundamental factors are necessary for habit formation. As we now know, habits are an intrinsic characteristic of human behaviour, helping us automate repetitive tasks to free up brain processing power. Nonetheless, some of our 'shortcuts' (habits) are undesirable, because they impact on our physical, mental and/or social health. Understanding the factors necessary for habit formation is very useful in learning how to break habits.

In behavioural psychology, a habit comprises three major elements: **repetition**, **automaticity** and **stable (consistent) contexts**[48,49]. Habitual behaviour is prompted by situational cues, repeated in a stable context[50].

When you perform an action for the first time, say driving a car, it requires mental effort and planning. It also requires paying attention to the behaviour. As you get more experienced in driving (you **repeat** the behaviour) and in the stable context (the same setting, which in this case, is your car), then the action becomes easier and more efficient each subsequent time that you do it (well, for some people, I see many drivers who seem not to have mastered some fundamental concepts of driving, such as how to use their indicators).

---

2 I actually know of someone who did break their leg cleaning their roof at 2am---no, I don't know why

After some time, the action becomes habitual, or **automatic**. You no longer have to think about changing gear (if you drive a stick shift) or what to do when merging into traffic. Some people seemingly lose all ability to think when they get in the car though; like the old joke, "a man is driving along on his usual route home, when his wife phones him, and says, 'honey, there's been a news item about some idiot driving the wrong way down the motorway'; he replies, 'it's not just one person, it's *hundreds* of them!'".

In addition, an important aspect of an action becoming habitual is in response to something that psychologists call a 'cue', or a specific situation, such as getting into a car and beginning to drive, or having a beer after work and lighting a cigarette.

Repetition

> "Habits are formed by the repetition of particular acts. They are strengthened by an increase in the number of repeated acts. Habits are also weakened or broken, and contrary habits are formed by the repetition of contrary acts." -**Mortimer J. Adler**

The more the behaviour is repeated in the same context, then the more likely it will become automatic, and thus a habit. Say you wake up on New Year's Day and decide to take up jogging. When your hangover fades, you lace up your new jogging shoes that your partner kindly (or sneakily) has bought you, and take to the street. Unless you are naturally athletic, or fit from other activities, your first attempt at running is usually a horrendous experience. Within minutes, your face turns bright red, your chest feels like you have been sat on by an elephant and a multitude of new and horrible physical symptoms appear.

If you are a hypochondriac, as I am, you soon realise that your death is imminent, and you stop, gasping, puffing, panting and retching. You then walk for five minutes before tentatively breaking into a run again---with the same result. Afterwards, you feel quite good---but the next day, every muscle is stiff and you hobble around in a wretched state. At the same time, your partner praises your pathetic attempts, and tells you that the best cure for muscle stiffness is---to go for a nice run (aka have one more of the one that bit you).

After some time (or some little time), it happens that the desire to go jogging is in indirect proportion to the effort it takes to actually get up and go for a run, then most will perform the behaviour only a few times before giving up. Thus, it is highly unlikely that, for them, jogging will become a habit. On the other hand, if the person keeps at jogging, and goes for a run every second day at the same time, every day it becomes easier, and it is more likely to become a habit.

Researchers have also found that there is a relationship between repeating an action and the strength of the habit. As an action is repeated more often, it becomes more automatic, until it reaches a plateau, where no further automaticity is possible. The longer the person performs that behaviour (or the greater the frequency of the past behaviour), the stronger the habit to perform that behaviour becomes. But this is not a linear relationship, with a straight line between repetition of an action and it becoming automatic.

Generally speaking, after a time or number of repetitions, the habit is now established, and further repetition will strengthen it, but not create a new habit. The 64 million dollar question is, how many repetitions over what time are needed to establish (or break) a habit? Is it the three months that is the staple of pop psychology or is it something else?

Complicating this of course, is that we are not computers, programmed to do something by simple action and response. A huge number of complex factors (variables) are involved in human behaviour, and these interact both within the person concerned (internal variables) and with outside variables (external or environmental variables).

What do I mean by that? Ok, Jane decides to take up jogging, and unlike some, she is very motivated, and wants her jogging to become a habit. However, Jane has genetically weak knees, and finds that jogging for more than a certain time causes her pain. This is an internal variable; and it might be addressed by choosing a different type of running shoe, or by substituting cycling for jogging. On the other hand, Jane has a young baby, works part time and lives in a cold area. Sometimes she desperately wants to go jogging, but cannot because she has no one to look after the baby, or the weather is too cold and wet. These are external or environmental variables.

Researchers have also discovered that more complex behaviour often has lower levels of habit, but they did not test how many repetitions were needed to create a habit from a complex behaviour. What do I mean by that? Let's look at the example of an Olympic level gymnast. Together with his coaches, and bearing in mind some specific requirements of the sport at that level, he will have created a set routine for each one of the six apparatus used in the discipline, such as floor, pommel horse and rings. Anyone who has ever seen these routines will acknowledge that they are incredibly complicated and difficult, requiring exceptionally high levels of skill and talent. BUT, they can also be considered a habitual activity, because flawlessly performing a complicated floor routine (or a ballet solo or piano concerto) is the result of many hours, weeks and years of practicing small actions over and over again, until each one is perfect, and then putting them together for the final routine.

Nonetheless, although aspects of complicated actions, such as a gymnastic routine, can be performed without thinking, they are not fully automatic, and require a good deal of what is known as goal-directed automaticity rather than habit. A highly complex action might never become habitual in the purest sense of the word, even if the essential component actions are habitual; for example, the specific movement of a gymnast in order to land at the end of a routine without hurting him or herself, as well as to 'stick' (land without falling or going over the line). But you would never see a gymnast mindlessly doing his routine in the middle of the street!

Therefore, an important part of habit formation is what is known as automaticity.

Automaticity of Habit

What exactly is automaticity in the context of behaviour? This might be behaviour that is efficient, unaware, unintentional and uncontrolled. Obviously many of these are not all that characteristic of human behaviour, no matter how habitual.

Automaticity is defined as---'the ability to do things without occupying the mind with the low-level details required, allowing it to become an automatic response pattern or habit. It's the result of learning, repetition, and practice'[51].

It has been suggested that automaticity can be further broken down into four sub features: **'lack of awareness, mental efficiency, lack of control, and lack of conscious intent'**[52].

Habits are also characterised by a lack of awareness, how many of us have gotten into our cars and driven somewhere, only to realise some time afterwards that many minutes or even hours have gone past without us being consciously aware of driving or the environment around us? This can be quite disturbing, but of course, our brains are perfectly aware, and if anything untoward were to happen, we'd immediately 'wake up'. Well, I hope so.

Secondly, as we saw in Chapter 3, our brains don't like to exert too much effort on cognitive processes that can be made automatic, and therefore require less effort. Imagine how complicated life would be if we had to think about everything we did? We probably wouldn't be able to do anything, because life would be such a huge effort.

Third, automaticity implies a lack of control. This sounds quite scary, but is quite common. For example, I've a bad habit of snacking after dinner, and if I drink wine, then I've even less control. I've often found myself snacking without even remembering getting up and going into the kitchen, preparing the snack or anything.

Lack of control also implies that giving up a habit can be extremely difficult, and requires constant mental intervention to break (how to break this cycle is detailed in chapter 5, how to use triggers to break habits). The brain constantly tries to force us back into the rut along the fence, and not the new path, which is more inconvenient and uncomfortable, and requires us to exert more effort.

Finally, lack of conscious intent. This is probably the defining reason for, and characteristic of habits. We form habits to save on conscious cognition. From cleaning our teeth, to driving our cars, we perform habitual behaviours without much, if any, conscious intent. How many times have you been walking to work or watching TV, and you suddenly think 'I can't remember what I did for the last ten minutes'. Obviously, if you are suddenly thinking this and you are upside down in a ditch, you were probably paying attention---just to the wrong thing, like texting your boyfriend. Nonetheless, you *were* paying attention but were just doing it automatically---out of habit.

Consciousness is hard work, most of our brain's work is done totally unconsciously; indeed as much as 98% of all our brains functioning is totally unconscious[53]. But we do use all of our brains, not just 10% like in myth!

Stable (consistent) context

A stable or consistent context is essential to habit formation, and this is because the fundamental basis of a habit is an action that is performed automatically, without thinking about it. If you drive to work every day in the same car at the same time on the same road (**consistent context**), that drive is likely to become a habit. Now, get in a new car, and drive in a city that you don't know, and see the difference. How many times have you hired a car and tried to indicate a turn and instead, turned on the windscreen wiper or the headlights? You habitually indicate on a certain side, depending on the car you drive. It normally takes at least a day or so to get used to using the indicators on the other side, and longer if you have had the previous car for some time.

If you have to take a different route to work every day, perhaps because you live in a really dangerous area, then you will probably never get habituated to the drive. You will be constantly paying attention to the world around you, in case, for example, there are suspicious looking cars, or signs warning of landmines or packs of ravening zombies to look out for. When I was younger, I lived in a country where there *was* the potential of landmines on the roads we drove to town or boarding school. There were also frequent ambushes of lone cars, and people were encouraged to drive in convoys. My father refused to drive in a convoy, so we had to look out for suspicious marks in the soil, as well as carry guns in case we were ambushed (his attitude was that if we shot back, they would run away). At 13, I fought with my younger sisters so I could sit behind my father, and to hold the *best* gun, a semi-automatic AR15 rifle

The complexity of behaviour

However, I am now going to throw few 'spanners in the works'.

Most early research on habit forming only investigated very simple behaviors and the simple habituation of performing those actions. For example, the researchers used subjects performing actions such as pressing levers or pulling strings, mostly because a lot of behavioural psychology was based on early research on the conditioning of animals. For example, Pavlov conditioned his dogs, by ringing a bell when food was served, and in time, the dogs salivated when the bell was rung, even though no food was produced. Other researchers included B F Skinner, who trained pigeons to peck a certain area to produce food. But humans are not animals and do not generally behave instinctively. Contemporary research highlights three types of habitual behaviour[54].

This is why breaking and making habits can be so difficult. Habitual behaviour is not always simple like in example three (and that is not that simple either); it is more often a combination of very complex actions, each of which is integral to the final behaviour.

Unfortunately, the sort of behaviour we want to encourage (healthy behaviour) is very often complicated rather than simple, and the habits we want to break in order to practice healthy behaviours, are rather pleasant. I love wine, so drinking it is pleasant. However, wine disagrees with me, and affects my sleep, which I also love; so there's a bit of a contradiction there.

And of course, the more complex the behaviour, the more steps that are required to perform it, and the more things that can go wrong. Riding my bicycle involves a number of small actions, such as unlocking my shed, taking the bicycle to the front yard, putting on my bike helmet and setting off. But what happens if my tire is flat, or I can't find the key to the shed? Then I might decide not to ride my bike, especially if I am running late and don't have the time to pump up the tire, or look for the key.

1. First is behaviour that is initiated habitually, but performed consciously, such as commuting. Say you habitually ride your bicycle to work rather than driving or taking the bus. But while the action of riding the bicycle is a habit, the action of riding to work is a complex behaviour and is not habitual. If you've been riding a bicycle for many years, you normally don't think about the process of riding a bicycle. So if your habit is to go to work every day by bicycle, unless you are running late, or it is raining, you will usually choose to ride rather than drive. On the other hand, the actual ride to work is not habitual. Every day's ride is different. Some days you meet people and chat, or swerve to avoid a dog or an aggressive road biker, or ride really fast to avoid being rained on, or if even to concentrate on the present experience.

2. Another type of habit is consciously initiated, but performed habitually. This might include going to the gym where you consciously think about going to the gym, if there is a class you wish to attend, what day and time the class occurs, and remember to bring gym clothes and a towel and to get to the gym. But once you are at the gym, you might do the same class every Wednesday or the same number of repetitions, which are habits.

3. Other types of habits are habitually initiated **and** performed. These habits are both easier and more difficult to give up, and are much simpler behaviours than the previous examples. For example, you could pour a glass of wine and drink it without thinking; or snack whilst watching TV.

In conclusion, I emphasize that human behaviour is NOT instinctive. We have a choice and 'free will' to change our response. No matter what our habits, we are not forced to behave in a certain way, even if it is an action that we have performed many times, without awareness, in a stable context. In other words, our behaviour is not a necessary consequence of encountering a cue for a habit. We can CHANGE our habitual behaviour[55].

CHAPTER 5 – THE PSYCHOLOGY OF CHANGING HABITUAL BEHAVIOUR

"To change a habit, make a conscious decision, then act out the new behavior." **Maxwell Maltz**

As we have seen, much of our behaviour can be considered habitual. This is because our brains don't like to expend too much effort on thinking about everyday things, so they create simpler, more automatic ways of doing things. Thus, when you create a habit, the neurons in your brain form a well-worn path, like Spot's rut alongside the fence.

But in order to change a habit or to start a new one, you have to dig the compacted dirt, put some fresh topsoil over, plant new grass, and ensure that Spot doesn't just start running along his old rut. Electric fences work well to prevent livestock doing this, but not that well for humans (and are probably illegal). I was once hiking in the French Pyrenees, and just about every fence had a sign saying 'Cloture Electrique' with a picture of someone getting a shock. After accidentally brushing a few of these, and not getting shocked, I then assumed that they were *all* turned off. Note; don't make assumptions, electric fences pack a mean punch!

Now, just as it's difficult for old dogs to change their ways, your brain resists any change to its habits because the energy from the food that we take in is mostly used (well for some of us) to keep our brains running nicely and smoothly. It takes a lot of energy to do many simple things, and the brain is lazy, it likes short cuts, so it can concentrate on the more important stuff, like keeping us alive.

Now, I'd hazard a guess and say that all of us have a collection of bad habits we want to get rid of, or some good habits, which we'd like to create.

However, it's extremely difficult to get rid of bad habits, and it's even more difficult when the bad habit is linked to a chemical addiction, such as drinking too much alcohol or smoking cigarettes.

It's also difficult when the good habit, say, taking up jogging, is painful, exhausting, and in the beginning, extremely unpleasant. Your body is quite happy on the couch, it doesn't want to go out in the sun and exert itself. Well, it's not happy, but you need to show it who is boss. That doesn't work with cats, by the way. Cats *are* the boss, and they know it, and will not hesitate to give you an 'affectionate' bite or clawing if you try and tell them otherwise.

But how do you get rid of your bad habits? It's all very well to say, ok, I want to cut down on drinking, stop smoking and take up jogging. It's like New Year's resolutions. This is impossible to quantify, but proportion of people who make resolutions, and keep them, is only about 8%. This isn't a large proportion. Most resolutions are broken in the first week, if not sooner. For me, the only New Year's resolution I ever kept was to drink only bottled and not box wine. Arguably, that is not a very difficult resolution. It's like saying; only eat Lindt chocolate and not 'no-name brand' chocolate. Unfortunately, my body has since declared war on me, and I have been forced to give up drinking (I know it's for my own good, but still, couldn't I have developed an intolerance to tomatoes, tripe or turnips, all of which I hate).

The same rule applies to diets. How many of you start diets, and break them almost immediately? I normally break my diets by lunch time; if not, then by the next day and almost always by the weekend. And as for cutting down on drinking---hmmm, Friday is a killer, and then if you have a drink on Friday, you may as well have one (yeah right) on Saturday, and Sunday too. And then, well Wednesday is the middle of the week, and you need a break, and if you drink on Wednesday, well it's not much point waiting until Friday, so you might just have one on Thursday too---.can you see where I'm going?

And what about good habits, like taking up jogging or going to the gym or writing every day? First, there's the gym rule, which I invented (or stole, sorry); namely, that the distance of the gym from your house is inversely proportional to the likelihood of you attending. If the gym is 200m down the road, and you go past it every day, you are way more likely to go than if it's 10km away, in a totally different direction to your work, the supermarket or your child's school. Mind you, there's a gym at my work, and I'm quite good at making excuses not to go. Nonetheless, **proximity and simplicity are key to creating habits.**

Also, it's not much point taking up some sort of exercise if you absolutely detest it. I loathe swimming in swimming pools as I'm allergic to chlorine, and I also hate swimming, unless it is in the ocean, on a dead calm summer day---which probably occurs 10 times a year, and even then, I'm afraid of sharks. Swimming is therefore not a suitable sport for me. Likewise, if you are very particular about looking neat and well groomed, you probably shouldn't take up jogging, especially if you live in a humid area. I live in a place called Brisbane, which is horrendously humid.

I have often seen people at the start of a marathon (one of the things that a masochist like me finds 'fun') wearing full makeup (beauty makeup, not like the charity or fun runners who dress up in gorilla suits or other odd outfits).No matter how waterproof it is, the makeup starts to run (unlike some of the wearers, who stop running) by about kilometer 5. And there's no way it will last until the marathon photographers take your picture. They are born sadists, who lurk almost at the finish, just at the top of the last hill, and take your picture just when you are looking your most unflattering, with tears running down your cheeks and with an expression on your face like a gorilla having an orgasm.

And as for giving up bad habits, that is even more difficult. There are genuine reasons why you begin certain habits. For example, you may have a really stressful job or a long commute or both, and you want to do nothing more when you get home than sit on the couch with a glass of red. And that is fine. It's just when you have two glasses, or three, and you do it every day, and then it becomes a bad habit. I used to binge drink when I was younger, but as I got older, I began to habitually drink. And the problem with habits, is that they sneak up so subtly. You start by say, having a glass of wine on a Friday night, and a year later, you're drinking two bottles a week. Well, it's normally a lot quicker with me, but I'm sure you get the picture.

Ok, but how DO we change behaviour? Especially when you are addicted to your habit, and it is just so nice!

HOW DO YOU CHANGE YOUR BEHAVIOUR?

> "Correcting bad habits cannot be done by forbidding or punishment." **Robert Baden-Powell**

A Marx (I don't recall which one, perhaps Groucho, but it sounds more like something Karl would say) but I can't find it in any quote dictionary, so I might have made it up, in which case, it is MINE©, once said, 'The only thing you can predict about human behaviour is that a person may do something, or they may not do it'. Human behaviour is inherently unpredictable.

There is a vast amount of academic and popular literature on behaviour change. The jobs of psychologists, marketers and advertisers, environmental scientists, political strategists and many others is to try and change human behaviour.

A cognitive psychologist may work to help overcome compulsive or fearful behaviour. Advertisers, marketers, retailers, restaurateurs, tourism operators and so on, constantly try and change behaviour to sell their products or services. Environmental scientists try to change behaviour so people use less water or electricity, or recycle their rubbish, or use the cold water cycle on their washing machines. Politicians try and change behaviour either by legislating for behaviour change (requiring new houses to install rainwater tanks or to install solar panels) or attempting to encourage behaviour change (using incentives such as rebates, or by running voluntary programs). In non-democratic nations, politicians may coerce people to change behaviour by threatening them or their families with violence, or legislating the types of behaviour they prefer.

When I grew up in Zimbabwe and South Africa, racism was entrenched in law, so that people of colour could not, for example, sit on the same bench as white people, or use the same toilets. In Australia (and places like the USA and the UK) certain racist politicians are discriminating against Muslim people, by using the media to incite fear and turn people against Muslims. This has resulted in a number of attacks on innocent people, based entirely on how they look or what they are wearing.

Essentially behaviour change strategies are either **prescriptive** (you will or will not do something, or else you will get punished) or **voluntary** (you have the **choice** to do it; if you choose not to do it, nothing will happen). As this book is not about forcing people to change their behaviour, it's only going to explore **voluntary** behavioural change. Besides, even when governments totally ban something, like alcohol during the US prohibition, or illegal drugs, humans usually find a way to get hold of the stuff. Then it raises the cost, so it becomes a more attractive good to sell, so then it's 'marketed', and so on---hence, making certain things, like drugs, illegal, without changing social attitudes towards them, is bound to fail.

However, **when social attitudes change**, it's often unnecessary to make something illegal. Usually, however, you need a combination of both. Take, for example, slavery. Slavery was undesirable in many ways, but even after it was banned, until people's attitudes changed, it still existed (sadly, it **still** exists in some countries). Still, one cannot judge historical trends with 21st century môres; in the past, people frequently had different attitudes to many subjects than they do now.

This is still relevant nowadays. I'm writing this from my own perspective, as an English speaking Caucasian, highly educated member of a developed nation; but it is important to note that attitudes to many things about which I write are totally different in other societies. For example, in many African societies, it's desirable for women to be overweight, which is of course, in direct contrast to many western countries. These attitudes are tending to become subsumed into western 'ideals' especially in cities, but are still relevant. Patriarchal and top-down attempts at changing others behaviour can often lead to backlash; after all, who are *'they'* to say that what *'I'* do is wrong?

So, there are a number of ways in which people can change their behaviour, or by which others can attempt to change the behaviour of others (much more difficult). Because this book is about habits, I am going to concentrate on behaviour change strategies that could be used to change **your OWN** habits, or give the information so you can get motivated (or at least intend) to change your habits.

Also, because habits are formed in consistent contexts, and in response to certain cues, I will also briefly discuss aspects of the environment in which habits are formed and continue. These topics include providing incentives and disincentives, information campaigns, fear-based campaigns, using triggers, mindfulness, vigilant control, using the principles of comfort, convenience and cost---and probably a thousand others.

I will begin with mass efforts to change behaviour (such as the habit and addiction to smoking tobacco) such as information campaigns, then the environment in which habits are formed, then discuss specifics to habit making and breaking.

Information Campaigns

It's common practice for organisations, governments, self-help groups, churches, medical practitioners and many others to try and help people break bad habits. For example, smoking is a major problem in many societies, and can have significant impacts on medical, social and economic outcomes of individuals and of society in general. For this reason, governments and health authorities attempt to intervene, by means of policy, to encourage people to give up smoking.

The most common method by which policy makers intervene to promote healthier behaviours is with information and awareness campaigns. These campaigns can take many forms, and include advertising in a range of media, educational resources, public campaigns, social media initiatives, websites and interactive multimedia, and even counselling with at risk individuals. Such campaigns may promote consulting a medical practitioner or using anti-smoking aids such as nicotine patches.

Another public health issue in many developed countries is increasing levels of obesity. Vast numbers of companies and marketers attempt to cash in on the lucrative weight-loss market, and the largely government-run campaigns promoting healthy dietary choices or increased exercise are matched with a plethora of advertising for one 'miracle' weight loss product or technique or other. Such private company marketing may be much more sophisticated than the government campaigns, and feature well-known celebrities or sports stars, glowing testimonials and slick marketing material.

But despite all the money spent on information campaigns, advertisements etc., most of these have little if any impact on actual behaviour. For example, some campaigns aimed at combatting substance abuse led, not to a decrease, but to an *increase* in the targeted behaviours, whilst conversely attitudes towards the substances changed to be more negative[56]. Other campaigns aimed at increasing condom use had little impact, and increases in general advertising did not increase sales.

Why are information campaigns so ineffective in changing habits, even if they do **succeed** in changing attitudes?

One simple reason is something called the attitude-behaviour gap, which means that no matter what a person's attitude to something, this often has little impact on their actual behaviour. This phenomenon is well known in behavioural psychology. Time and again, an intervention will significantly change attitudes, but behaviours obstinately remain the same. Thus, a range of variables prove significant for *intention* to behave, but have very little relevance to the actual behaviour.

Some reasons for this are purely situational. For example, John might have a positive attitude towards reducing greenhouse gas (GHG) emissions, so instead of driving to work, he intends to reduce emissions and improve his fitness by riding his bicycle. However, on rainy days, or when he's running late, then his very strong intention (and his beliefs and attitudes) are easily overcome by the desire to save time, and maintain his comfort and convenience (by not cycling in the rain). Frequently, what happens is that a person such as John will start to form a positive habit (cycling to work instead of taking the car) and the times when it's inconvenient start to outweigh the times that he actually performs the action. Months go by, and John's bicycle is mouldering in the garage, and his car is the only thing that is getting a workout.

In addition, information and education campaigns are what are called downstream interventions. They aim to change the habitual behaviour of people who **already** have a bad habit, whether this is drinking too much alcohol, smoking or eating too much junk food. They are also aimed at changing the habits of **individuals**. So why are downstream interventions ineffective?

The reason for this goes back to the origin of habit formation. As we saw, habits are created when we repeat behaviour in consistent stable contexts, usually in response to environmental, social, emotional and other cues. Therefore, downstream interventions, such as providing awareness of the health risks of behaviour such as smoking, do not address the complex context and factors under which the habit was originally formed.

When a person first learns a new habit (let's use the driving analogy) they decide what to do, learn new information and techniques for doing so, and practice the behaviour repeatedly. So Jane decides to get her driver's license, studies for her learners permit, and practices driving until she's confident enough to get her license. Being able to drive also has a variety of incentives; Jane is free to go where she pleases, she can meet her friends, and she can get a job further afield, and she feels good to be an independent adult.

But, as Jane repeats her actions, say by driving on the same road every day to work, her actions become habitual, and she does not make conscious decisions about this, unless the environmental cues change dramatically (for example, someone has an accident or the road is flooded). Generally though, the road is the same, and even the cars are often the same. That is why, after some time, Jane gets to work every day, sometimes without even remembering the drive. *Forming habits involves creating associations in memory between actions and stable features of the circumstances in which they are formed*[57].

Why habits are resistant to information campaigns

In the beginning of habit formation, people learn to develop expectations about the result of their behaviour. For example, if your habit is to have a glass of wine at a certain time every day, you look forward to and expect the relaxed sensation and the pleasant taste and learn to link this with returning home, perhaps after a hard day at work and endless traffic jams on the highway.

Because this is a habit, it's based on repetition in a similar context. Still, habits are quite resistant to small changes in the environment. For example, if you drink a large glass of red wine every night, you are unlikely to notice that the government has forced the winemaker to add a disclaimer on the bottle about the harmful effects of excess alcohol (particularly if it is printed in yellow 6 point font on a beige background). Nor is it likely that the average wine drinker will notice whether their favourite tipple has 13, 13.5 or 14% alcohol; information which is legally required to be printed on every bottle of wine sold.

Thus, an information campaign aimed to showing new information to people about potentially harmful activities (i.e. drinking too much, smoking cigarettes etc.) might not even be noticed by the people to whom it's targeting. Even if it IS noticed, it's also common that it will be discounted as irrelevant, or evidence of a government attempt to control personal freedom.

Another problem is that people with strong habits tend to make decisions based on less information than those with weaker habits. Someone with a strong habit to eat snack foodsmay decide to buy this food based on their favourite brand, or what is on special, and ignore the mandatory nutritional information, like the proportion of trans-fat, sugar or GMOs.

Moreover, even if they do read the nutritional information, they are likely not to take any notice of the suggested serving size, which is often a much smaller proportion, than the entire packet (the serving size that the person is most likely to eat). It's the same for alcohol, how many people, apart from bartenders at the stingiest pubs, take any notice of the standard serving, which is only 100mm, and is much smaller than an average wine glass?

This also means that people with strong habits are less likely to investigate all the options available when making a decision, unlike those with weaker habits. For example, if you do not have a strong habit to eat snack foods, and are looking to buy some potato crisps for a child's party or other social occasion, you may well look at the nutritional information on each packet when deciding which brand to buy. Because buying and consuming such products is not part of your habitual behaviour, you are much more likely to notice such things as saturated or trans-fat percentages, or alcohol warnings. However, if you normally buy these every day, you are much more likely just to buy your usual brand, or a similar brand that is on special.

Also, searching for information on a habitual action is largely related to confirmation bias, people generally seek out information to support their usual choices. Someone who habitually drives might only use Google Maps to seek information on getting to the shops by car, and wouldn't even think of ticking the cycling, public transport or walking options.

This can be seen in a more subtle way, with unhealthy behaviours. For example, if you like to drink a couple of glasses of wine a day, information in the media on the health benefits of wine is likely to be noticed much more readily than information on the damaging health impacts of alcohol. Even if the article on the benefits of wine mentions aspects such as the benefits of wine in small regular servings (for example, no more than two 100mm glasses of wine per day for women, and never more than 14 alcohol units per week) and that drinking more than that is linked to an increased risk for chronic disease such as certain types of cancer or liver disease, the habitual drinker may discount the negative information in favour of the positive information. Drinking wine is good for the health, cheers. That's why I gave so much negative information on alcohol in the beginning of this book ;-).

'Upstream' interventions to break habits

As an alternative to downstream interventions (i.e. attempting to break a habit that is already well established), there are also upstream interventions. These are aimed to **prevent** habits forming and undesirable outcomes of these; such as improving the efficiency and availability of public transport and requiring additional checks and balances before the sale of potentially harmful products such as cigarettes and alcohol.

Thus, while downstream interventions are generally aimed at the individual; upstream interventions are generally conducted on the large scale and aimed at entire populations. There are many types of upstream incentives, including policies to change the environment in which behaviour occurs, marketing of alternatives, economic measures such as taxes or fines, and education and awareness campaigns.

First, policies aimed at changing the environment or the technology that supports the undesirable behaviour are common upstream interventions. These are not only used to prevent undesirable health behaviour, but to encourage positive habits in other aspects, such as sustainable transport choices, recycling, and as part of demand-side measures, for example, to reduce the excess use of water and energy. These might include mandatory rainwater tanks in new houses, phasing out of incandescent light bulbs, and requirements for low flow shower heads or dual flush toilets.

This type of behaviour change is different to behaviour that results from the mere intention to change, and almost completely under volitional control. Such behaviour has been termed 'curtailment' and includes **personally choosing** to reduce water use by taking shorter showers, or drinking alcohol only on weekends[58]. On the other hand, upstream behaviour changes can also be moderated by 'efficiency measures', such as reducing water use because of flow restricting devices or a festival that only sells light beer. These are therefore not under full volitional control (unless of course, the person gets annoyed at the lower flow, and removes the device or sneaks in some vodka into the festival in a Wine Rack, aka a fake bra with a container for alcohol[59]).

Other ways in which policy measures can help to change the environment include requirements for bicycle lanes on certain roads, residential subdivisions designed to encourage walking and the use of public transport, increasing land density in urban areas, and transport oriented development, where multiple use developments are created around transport hubs. In health, these policy measures can include the banning of smoking in some public places, or the banning of soft drinks in school canteens, restrictions on alcohol advertising at sporting events, only serving low alcohol beer at some sporting events, providing free condoms at university parties such as spring break, or free public transport after major events. In general, these are put into place by government agencies or educational institutions, and can often be quite costly to implement.

Secondly, are economic measures, such as the use of taxes, incentives, fines and subsidies[60]. There is some indication that economic incentives can have a small positive impact on forming good habits. Economic incentives are an example of extrinsic motivation, and when providing these, policy makers or others run the risk of the habit returning when the incentive ends.

Many years ago, my father once bought international air tickets for my sister and myself, in exchange for giving up smoking. We readily took the tickets, and when we got on the plane (I did say it was a long time ago), the first thing we did when we were permitted, was light up a cigarette!

However, in a couple of studies looking at providing incentives for students to go to the gym, economic incentives proved to be quite useful at least, in the initial motivation. Of three groups of students, the group who received a one-off payment to attend the gym increased their attendance compared to the first group who received no payment, but the group who received a further incentive for continuing to attend the gym increased their gym visits by the most. Of course, students do not usually have a lot of money, so this may not work with other groups. Also, when investigating the gym attendance of all these students after the break, no group had any significant gym attendance, showing that the habit lasted only as long as the incentive.

Other economic incentives and disincentives include subsidies for desired behaviours, or negative interventions, such as 'sin taxes' on alcohol, tobacco or gambling. Congestion pricing is another example of this, where people driving into a city are charged more or less money at different times of the day.

Finally, education campaigns are usually targeted at schoolchildren, and places where young people, have not yet formed a habit, or are only in the early stages of habit formation. Weaker habits are easier to break than strong habits. If children for example, do not start smoking or get in the habit of regular exercise, they are more likely to continue as they get older (peer pressure aside).

However, although upstream measures can help break habits without much requirement for thinking, they are large scale, and can be extremely expensive for a government to implement. They can also require major changes in legislation, policy and manufacturing. Thus, this sort of intervention is generally only used in significant issues, which may not be those for which people want to break habits. Yes, they are used in alcohol and tobacco use, but as both of those are habits practiced by individuals, it's difficult to devise upstream interventions, at least to curtail the habit after it has become established.

Why appeals to fear don't work to change habits

A common type of information campaign used by governments and marketers is what is known as an 'appeal to fear' or a fear-based campaign. These were based on research by Carl Hovland in the early 1950s, who developed something called the *Drive Reduction Model of persuasion and attitude change*. The underlying principle was that fear was considered a drive state (or motivational process), and that fear appeals or campaigns that triggered this state, would motivate the recipient to seek to reduce their fear by changing their behaviour.

'A fear appeal is a persuasive communication attempting to arouse fear in order to promote precautionary motivation and self-protective action'[61].

These campaigns been widely used (with very little change) for over 60 years, and are commonly used in attempts to change behaviour, such as health behaviour (i.e. smoking and unsafe levels of drinking), traffic behaviour (i.e. dangerous driving), and environmental behaviour (i.e. climate change).

Fear is an emotion that is triggered by an actual or perceived threat, external stimuli, learned behaviour and even instinct. Fear results in physiological arousal, and is generally considered an unpleasant emotion. It's assumed that the majority of people will do all they can to alleviate the threat and reduce the fear. For example, when faced with a poisonous snake in the house, people might do a number of different actions, such as run away, kill it, chase it away, or call a snake catcher. Fear appeals basically provide information; on the threat, and how to get rid of the threat.

First, they attempt to provide information that will initiate or arouse fear of something, which may or may not be already considered a threat. For example, in the early days of HIV/AIDS, fear campaigns presented HIV as a threat, to which people having unprotected sex were vulnerable, and which potentially had severely negative consequences, i.e. debilitating illness, infecting loved ones, and eventual death. Second, they present information to motivate people to engage in **simple behaviours** to negate or ameliorate the threat. For example, using condoms during intercourse can prevent the transmission of HIV. Some types of fear appeals are quite confronting, and rely on what is known as 'shock tactics' which are highly emotive techniques, such as showing pictures of motor vehicle accidents and victims, diseased organs on cigarette packets, or people dying of starvation.

The success (or not) of fear based campaigns relies on three factors: fear, perceived threat and perceived efficacy. First, fear is an unpleasant emotional state that is triggered by an emotional stimulus, which may be an actual or perceived threat, a learned behaviour or habit. Fear is triggered by the release of chemicals in the brain which then lead to physiological arousal, with symptoms such as increases in breathing and heart-rate, muscle tension, stomach distress and so on. The fear response is almost completely automatic, and is commonly known as the 'fight or flight mechanism'. It's a deep and atavistic instinct, which every creature has, and is intended to help you survive danger by either defending yourself (fight) or running away (flight).

Second, fear campaigns rely on perceived threats, and these have two dimensions, susceptibility and severity of the threat. Unlike fear, which is entirely emotional; whether you evaluate something as a threat (or not) is a cognitive and intellectual process. Nonetheless, they are related; if you think something is a severe threat, you will experience greater levels of fear.

For example, if you have a phobia about snakes, you will likely evaluate *any* snake, no matter how harmless, as a threat, and thus experience extreme fear. When faced with a snake in the home (susceptibility to the threat) and degree of existing phobia (severity of the threat), a person with a phobia about snakes will likely behave in an extreme manner which is unrelated to the actual threat posed by the snake.

Finally, perceived efficacy (also similar to perceived behavioural control in some behavioural frameworks) also has two dimensions; perceived self-efficacy and perceived response efficacy. Perceived self-efficacy relates to whether or not a person **believes** they have the ability to undertake an action. For example, if you believe that giving up drinking will be extremely difficult, then you will be less likely to respond to anti-drinking campaigns. Perceived response efficacy means the belief whether your **response** will alleviate the threat. For example, if you don't believe that giving up drinking will improve your health, or that it causes chronic illness, you are unlikely to give up.

Despite their almost ubiquitous use in contemporary society, there is relatively poor empirical evidence that fear-based campaigns change behaviour in the direction intended. Indeed, recent research indicates that these might trigger the **opposite** response, which may negate their message, or even backfire, with the result that people may increasingly practice the negative behaviour, instead of seeking to change it. This is because people have a psychological defense mechanism against fear, which can result in denial, ridicule, neutralization, or minimization. On the other hand however, some may indeed adopt the recommendation of the message, and change their behaviour accordingly. However, research shows that frequently these do not work, and may instead lead to defense of one's position and denial[62]

Another means by which the psychology of habit formation (and habit breaking) is to look into the environment in which the habit occurs; if a desired behaviour, such as going to a gym, is uncomfortable, inconvenient and expensive, then it is not going to become a habit.

Comfort, cleanliness and cost

A ground-breaking study by Professor Elizabeth Shove[63] highlighted that changing behaviour is more likely to occur if it does not impact on comfort, cleanliness (convenience) and cost. This has been applied mostly in the field of environmental behaviour, but is also relevant for habit breaking (and making). In societies where natural resources are readily accessible, such as a reliable source of freshwater from household taps, or electricity at the flick of a switch, it's quite common for people to waste such resources.

In rural areas, particularly those without access to reticulated water supplies, householders are always aware when supplies are running low (the dam levels are dropping) or the quality is worsening (the dam is covered in algae, or you can see---and smell---a dead cow in it). But our modern urban society has developed a complex, yet invisible supply of water supply and distribution, with little if any connection with the source of supply, so urban householders ('end-users' in government speak) have no idea of the quantity or quality of the resource. There could be an entire herd of dead cows in the dam, and unless you get sick, you wouldn't have a clue.

There's many a true story about rooftop water tanks having dead things in them for weeks, including people, such as the creepy tale of Elisa Lam, who was filmed getting into a lift, seemingly terrified of some unknown and invisible pursuer, and then being found dead a week later in a rooftop water tank[64]. Back to water. In most of our cities, at the turn of a tap, households can access seemingly endless and highly convenient supplies of cheap clean water. This is also known as the 'tragedy of the commons' where if a resource is (almost) freely available to all, people will not conserve it[65].

So what has this got to do with habits? Well, in keeping with the water theme, let's look at teeth cleaning or hand-washing. Both are "good" habitual behaviour. These are taught in childhood, both by parents and schools. Having water at the touch of a tap is convenient, having hot or cold water is comfortable, and it's relatively cheap, hence cost.

So what happens when you try and break the habit, say of letting the tap run whilst brushing your teeth? It's wasteful to let the tap run, and uses surprisingly large amounts of water. But it's hard to stop doing so, when it's habitual behaviour. You have to constantly monitor yourself, so that if the tap is running, to tell yourself to turn it off. It's inconvenient to do this all the time.

Ok, so what about driving? Say you want to cycle to work instead of driving. Currently, it's relatively cheap to drive, it's convenient and it's comfortable. Cycling may well be cheaper, but it certainly can be inconvenient and uncomfortable, especially you live far away from work, in a very hilly area, there is nowhere to cycle except on busy roads, and the weather is bad. Unless cycling can be made more convenient and comfortable, say by moving closer to work, or you have very strong motivations to cycle, say you are training for a major race, it's unlikely that it will become a strong habit. It's all too easy to slip back into your old habits. One day you might drive to work, because you think it's going to rain, then in a few weeks' time, you might find that you are driving to work every day, just like before, and the bike is mouldering in the garage.

This principle can apply to any number of habits that you wish to cultivate. Say you wake up one morning and decide to join a gym to get fit. But you can't find a gym close to home, so you find one about 10km away. You might go to the gym religiously for the first week, but by the second week or so, you start getting irritated by the traffic, the fact that you can't go to the gym except at peak times, so you have to wait for machines and the classes are all full, and before you know it, you stop going to the gym. Some unscrupulous gyms make a lot of money by churning customers this way. But what if you have a gym next door to your house, or at your workplace? Well, that is much more convenient, you can go at lunch times or even earlier in the morning. In that case, you are much more likely to continue the habit.

In psychological research, making things easier is called an efficiency intervention, and these are often very effective in preventing the formation of undesirable habits, and also for minimising some impacts of existing habits. In the case of water use, these might include flow restricting devices on showers, dual flush systems on toilets, or a requirement for washing machines to have minimum water efficiency standards. These work very well because they don't impact our comfort. There is little difference if any in the subjective enjoyment of an eight minute shower under full water pressure or one under lower water pressure (well, my son once called this equivalent to standing in a shower in an alley with someone spitting on you once a minute, but they have improved since then). And as for washing machines, many of the newer more efficient machines are more effective at washing than the older, wasteful machines.

For drinking, there is a basic efficiency intervention that you can do, and that is to not buy alcohol. If there is no alcohol in the house, and it is inconvenient to go and buy some more, then you are less likely to drink. One way I used to do this, before giving up drinking entirely, was when I got home, I'd walk my dog, then have a bath and get into my pajamas. If I wanted wine, I would then have to change (I'm no fashionista, but not *that much* of a slob, lol), get in my car, and drive to the bottle shop. Even though it is relatively close to my house, it was almost always far too much hassle---and then, before I knew it, I didn't feel like drinking anyway.

However, if a desired change requires something that's uncomfortable and inconvenient, then it's likely to fail. Changes are most effective when they do not involve major reductions of comfort, cleanliness and convenience. Take water use again; a person wishes to save water, and cuts down their daily showers, not flushing the toilet or washing clothes by hand in the bath, these attempts will likely fail, likely because their loved ones will complain about the smell---and will not result in any long term behaviour change.

This is because they counter social norms of comfort, cleanliness and convenience. Cutting down on showering obviously impacts on your personal hygiene, especially in summer or after exercising, and having stale (not to mention, smelly) sweat is itchy and uncomfortable, and having to listen to your partner and/or colleagues complaining is annoying.

Not flushing the toilet after urinating might save significant quantities of water, and possibly could be maintained in a very small household, but in a large household, could get very smelly, very quickly. Leaving urine to stay in the toilet bowl also stains the porcelain, and is difficult to clean; and not flushing after defecation is just gross. Thus this counters our norms of cleanliness. Washing clothes by hand is also difficult, time consuming, and could lead to back injury from incorrectly lifting heavy wet garments. This is inconvenient, and is unlikely to become part of habitual behaviour. It also counters norms of cleanliness and comfort, as hand washing is less efficient, and the clothes can be hard and prickly.

How could this be relevant to drinking? Well, we can see that making it inconvenient to drink (by having no booze in the house) is a useful trick. But how could giving up also be considered inconvenient or uncomfortable? Well, this might apply in social situations, particularly those with people who drink a lot and who are used to *you* drinking a lot, with them. They might (and frequently do), make it very uncomfortable to socialise with them, as they constantly pressurise you to drink---because most people don't like their friends to change too much, and also because you not drinking makes *them* feel uncomfortable. In this case, you might want to cut down on the amount that you socialise with them, change the socialising times (from evenings to morning coffee for example), or volunteer to be the designated driver.

So, we must ensure that to break a bad habit or create a good habit, that it is something that does not impact too severely on our comfort (say a sedentary person beginning a fitness regime by training for a marathon), convenience (joining a gym that is across town from where you live) or cost (taking up an extremely expensive sport, such as polo or cross-country skiing in a hot climate). Also, we need to look at how to maintain the good habit or not doing the bad habit, and one way to do this is to provide incentives and disincentives.

Incentive and disincentive.

One of the commonest methods for breaking habits is providing incentives or rewards. However, it's important to differentiate between extrinsic (external) rewards, such as financial incentives; and intrinsic (internal) rewards, such as the feeling of achievement that you gain from succeeding in a goal, such as reducing your daily drinking to only three times a week (though of course, not binging on those three days). External rewards can also be differentiated into whether they will be given on completion of the behaviour (i.e. giving up drinking for Dry July), on attainment of a specific standard (i.e. reducing drinking to only a certain number of alcohol units per week) or another outcome after the performance (i.e. maintaining a non-drinking regime over a difficult time, such as New Year).

However, while external incentives for breaking or making habits can work in some cases; in other cases, it can be counterproductive, and can work in the opposite way intended. If behaviour is only practiced because of an anticipated reward, as soon as that reward is taken away, it is often abandoned. It's impractical to reward yourself every time you do something. For example, if you reward yourself with a large chocolate each time you don't drink, not only will this lead to a new habit, it will probably make you put on weight too---and then you may feel depressed about being overweight, and start drinking again.

Also, if you think about it, if you want to make something into a habit and every time you practice that behaviour, you reward yourself, it's never going to become habitual, because you only do it anticipating a reward. The best extrinsic rewards are unexpected, and are proportional to the behaviour. For example, if every time little Johnny paints a picture, no matter what the quality, he gets a certificate and a medal, he's not going to improve his painting, and soon he's going to get bored with the rewards, so that they become meaningless. However, if he paints a particularly good picture, and enters it in a competition, and wins the prize for best picture, out of hundreds of other entrants, then this is going to motivate him to work harder at his painting.

On the other hand, intrinsic rewards can be very powerful in making or breaking habits, and do not become stale, as do extrinsic rewards. For example, if Joan decides to give up drinking, and every time she manages to go without a drink, she feels a sense of achievement, and at the same time, starts to sleep better and not have a headache in the morning, then these intrinsic rewards build up, positively reinforcing her new behaviour. One way in which she might do this, is instead of having a drink, do something else pleasurable, like going for a walk in the park, or having a really nice cup of tea or a non-alcoholic cocktail. After doing this, she's less likely to want a drink, and more likely to feel good about herself. Positive reinforcement is very powerful.

The calendar (as well as the related Seinfeld Chain) method which I describe later is a wonderful example of an intrinsic reward. The more that you stick to your goals, the more stars or symbols you get on the calendar, the less you are inclined to break your run. This really works! It works even better if your calendar is in a public place, so that your family or housemates can see it.

So, what about disincentive? Disincentives are not as good as incentives, and may backfire, but can also be used as tools for habit control. A disincentive is basically a punishment that either you, or someone else, doles out to you if you lapse. For example, you could set up a system of fines, where if you drink, you put some money in a jar. Another way is to put aside a relatively large sum of money, and each time you lapse, you lose a certain amount. This works as both an incentive (you get the money at the end) and a disincentive (if you lapse, you get less money).

However, people are complicated creatures, and often if you punish them, or make them feel bad about themselves, it does not necessarily result in a good outcome. Just look what happens when you go on a diet. You are starving (often literally, depending on the faddiness of the diet) and sooner or later, temptation will rear its ugly head, and you will lapse. Now, instead of just saying, 'oh poop, I broke my diet' and using it as a lesson that perhaps your diet is too strict or restrictive, it is common then to completely rebel and go on a huge binge. So now, instead of eating one ice cream cone, you go out and buy a whole tub, and while you are about it, a packet of Doritos. And if you get someone else to enforce your rewards and punishments, I almost guarantee that it is going to result in conflict.

As you can figure, I am not really in favour of disincentives as a way to make or break habits.

But no matter how many rewards you give yourself, a habit is something that is by its nature mindless. You have to find some way of making that habit mindful, and this is called vigilant control.

Vigilant control

A recent study found that a large proportion of those people who successfully broke bad habits used a technique called 'vigilant control'[66,67]. What is vigilant control? Because habits are largely automatic and mindless, breaking them requires **paying attention** to what you are doing. Those who were most successful in breaking their bad habits thought things like 'don't do it' and watched themselves carefully for any lapses. Self-regulation is particularly useful in helping to break bad habits and to form new good habits. Interestingly, the study found that this was the only method that helped change strong and persistent habits.

It is important to differentiate between temptation control, distraction and vigilant control, as they are all different. Temptations are not habits; for example, a buffet full of lovely snacks at a function is a temptation to break one's diet, but eating these (or lots of these) is not a habit.

You can control temptations by removing the temptation, removing yourself, or distracting yourself. Distraction is also useful in certain circumstances, but not in eliminating or creating a habit.

Someone who is prone to mindless snacking needs to concentrate on what he or she is doing, and **not** become distracted. Habits are **unconscious**, and they thrive on distraction. Also, habits are triggered because of cues in the environment, which may not be immediately obvious. For example, a certain aspect of the environment might be a cue for a specific habit, such as sitting on your chair on the deck which cues your desire to have a drink after work.

Researchers used two samples, in the first, 99 undergraduate students (61 female and 38 male) who participated as part of the requirements for their degree, and in the second phase, another 33 students participated for a payment of $40. The participants attended various group sessions, which included a lecture on how people change their thoughts, feelings and behaviours. They also received printed diaries and over a 7-day period had to record the listed behaviours that they wanted to change or inhibit (reduce). They had to carry the diaries with them at all times, and within 15 minutes of their action, write what had happened and if it was successful.

The students had to write down every habit they wanted to inhibit or change, and the second group listed habits they wanted to start. Behaviours included not overeating, and not sleeping during lectures (well, they were students—although perhaps the lecturers were to blame). The first group tried to inhibit behaviours and the second to change their behaviour. They also had to write down if they tried to inhibit or change a specific behaviour and if it had not worked. Students also had to report to the lab every 2 or 3 days to report their progress, in what were called 'continuation sessions'.

They had to tick the strategies used to stop themselves doing the habit. These strategies had already been worked out in pretesting, and included; a) vigilant monitoring *'thinking 'don't do it' or watching carefully for mistakes'* and monitoring; *'(b) distracting myself; (c) stimulus control of removing myself from the situation or removing the opportunity to do it; or (d) nothing—I did not try to stop this time'*

The study found that **vigilant monitoring was highly successful in controlling habits**, particularly strong habits. Distracting themselves or removing themselves from the area was not as successful, especially as people were not particularly good at identifying what cued their habits.

In a contrary finding to 'common sense', distraction wasn't particularly successful in either breaking habits or stopping behaviour when faced with temptations. Also, the degree of motivation of the subjects had little significance; it was the vigilant monitoring that was so successful---*whether the students were motivated to change or not.* Also interesting, is that monitoring was no more successful than any other method used to deal with weak habits.

So why does vigilant monitoring work so well in helping break habits---and most importantly, in breaking strong habits? The major reason is because it encourages or heightens 'conscious control processes' which are the primary method of overriding habits[68]. Because habits are automatic and triggered by cues in the environment, actively encouraging conscious awareness is key to combatting the automaticity of habit.

The most important part of the calendar technique is based on vigilant monitoring. One way to practice vigilant control is to practice mindfulness.

Mindfulness

A method to increase conscious control and awareness (i.e. vigilant monitoring) is mindfulness. As we have repeatedly seen, when you are distracted, then you are more likely to lapse. Habits are automatic, and thrive on distraction.

Mindfulness is very 'in', but beyond all the hype and celebrity endorsements, it is extremely useful, particularly in breaking habits (also for helping with mild anxiety and depression). I'll give a brief overview of what mindfulness is, with respect to habits, and share a few techniques to improve your own mindfulness.

So, what is mindfulness[69]? Many people think it synonymous with meditation, or with Buddhism, but although it originated in these philosophies, it is different. Mindfulness means paying attention or using techniques to become more aware of what is going on in the present. It is **not** emptying your mind (nor is meditation for that matter). Mindfulness has five interrelated aspects; awareness, observing, describing, non-reacting and non-judging[70].

So why should you practice mindfulness (apart from wanting to break or make habits)[71]? Many studies have demonstrated the benefits of mindfulness, and some are summarized below (based on the website in the footnote).

Health benefits (for both physical and mental health). Mindfulness benefits our immune systems, helps with depression and anxiety, has been effective in reducing the symptoms of PTSD, increases the density of grey matter in the brain, reduces negative emotions such as stress whilst boosting positive emotions, can help fight excessive drinking or eating by making people more aware of mindless consumption.

Emotional benefits. Mindfulness can increase our empathy, help us focus and tune out distractions, improve our memory, learning and attention skills, it increases compassion, altruism and empathy and also self-compassion, and it reduces anger, hostility and other negative emotions. If negative emotions are reduced, then we are less likely to turn to alcohol to soothe our stress or sorrow.

Social benefits: Mindfulness can improve relationships, helping couples become more satisfied with their relationship, improving optimism, relaxation and closeness; it is good for parents and expectant mothers, reducing anxiety, stress and depression, and improves relationships with children; it is used in schools to reduce behavioural issues such as aggression and improve happiness and ability to pay attention, and teachers also greater compassion and empathy and lower stress and depression. Mindfulness also helps doctors and nurses deal with stress and anxiety, improve their quality of life and pass these skills on to their patients. It is used in prisons to reduce aggression, hostility and other disturbances, and help with rehabilitation.

Awareness (or concentration): paying attention and being fully present in whatever you are doing. As we have learned, this is the exact opposite of habitual behaviour. How much of our day do we actually pay attention to? Some of us pay very little attention to little in our daily lives. We spend so much time looking at screens, that our awareness of the world around is becoming even more limited.

Observing: linked to awareness, it means to observe both your external and internal world. What are the feelings and thoughts going through your mind, what are the sounds, smells and sights around you? Learning to observe like this gives you greater insight into your own mental world, and cast a fresh new light on the world around you. As a child, I was delighted watching vegetable seeds that I had planted begin to come up and the delicacy of the new leaves. That is a beautiful feeling, that joy.

Describing: This basically means exactly what it says, naming your experiences in simple words. Even if you are not a writer, working at describing internal and external sensations is a useful practice. I used to live under a flight path of a busy city airport and every day I heard aeroplanes overhead. What is the noise that they make? I could just say, 'planes', but each one is different, something I particularly notice when the huge A380 flew low over my house, and everything rattled.

Non-reacting: This is a regular New Year's resolution for me. I am working at not 'going off' if I read something online, or hear something that I disagree with, particularly in a field in which I am a (relative) expert. I am also prone to extreme clumsiness, and when I hurt myself, jump up and down and scream and yell, in a manner quite unbecoming. Non-reacting on the other hand means to just 'let it go'.

Non-judging: This is essentially what it says, awareness, observing, describing, non-reacting and then non-judging. What does that mean? Well, judging something or someone is often based on learned associations throughout one's life, and is usually totally incorrect. For example, I grew up in apartheid South Africa, and we were taught many evil and incorrect things about other people, just because they had different skin colour, and it took me years to unlearn all the indoctrination from authorities, friends, the media and even family. Of course, not all judging is as bad as racism, but just think back to last time you saw an overweight person, or a smoker, or someone with a lot of tattoos---frequently we judge a person based solely on their appearance, which is quite cruel, and usually wrong. And we also judge ourselves, and sometimes that can be the worst of all.

So, how do you practice mindfulness? Well, how long is a piece of string? There are thousands of different mindfulness practices. I'm not going to go into many of these, as you can find heaps on the internet, but here are some techniques that can be used (and some of which I use to cope with my own anxiety and stress). First are some basic principles:

- Pay close attention to your **breathing**, especially if you are feeling emotional. This helps you deal with the triggers (or cues) of life
- Try and really pay attention to what your **senses** are telling you; the sights, sounds, smells and sensations around you (and inside)
- Understand that what you are **feeling**, your thoughts and emotions, are fleeting, and don't define who you are, and if you think negative things about yourself, they are not true.
- Try and concentrate on the **physical sensations** of your body, the feeling of the sun on your skin, or how your legs feel when you have been standing or sitting for a long time.

Here is a short mindfulness practice on drinking (link to an interesting video on mindful eating in the footnotes; the principles are the same for drinking)[72]. Many of us, including myself, tend to drink or eat mindlessly, whilst doing other stuff, like watching TV or checking our Facebook feed. In this way, we drink too fast, are not aware of our body telling us we have had enough, and do not savour what we are drinking. Drinking mindlessly has many negative consequences, including getting drunk, drinking too much, and doing things like mindless snacking or drunk texting or internet shopping.

Obviously, if you are trying to give up drinking entirely, substitute the wine for some lovely non-alcoholic drink, like fresh mint tea, or sparkling (unfermented) grape juice.

This is a basic mindfulness eating exercise, but will help you become more aware of when you are drinking mindlessly. In the developed world, we are extremely privileged by the amount, quality and access to food and drink that we have. Many others do not have the same freedoms. We should be grateful for what we drink and eat, for our mother earth, and for how it sustains our body. Drinking mindfully will help you appreciate what you are drinking, even if you just appreciate that you have access to clean, fresh water (which many in the world do not). Eating mindfully will also help you choose food with high nutritional value, rather than junk food, full of salt, sugar and saturated fat.

The basic tenet of this is to drink (or eat) without distractions. Sit down, turn off the TV, put away your phone, book or iPad and concentrate on your food. This is very difficult, but well worth the effort.

Mindfulness drinking exercise[111]

For this I will use wine, but you can use it for any drink (including non-alcoholic drinks). The principles are the same for wine tasting!

Intention: First, set your intention for drinking mindfully. Ask yourself, am I drinking to ease stress, because I like the taste or to drown my sorrows?

Holding: First, open the wine slowly, and pour it into a clean wine glass. Hold the wine glass in your hand, tilt it against the light or a white surface, and look at the colour of the wine. Focus on it, and imagine that you've never seen something like this before in your life.

Seeing: Take time to really see the wine, gaze at the drink with care and full attention. Let your eyes explore every part of it, examining the highlights where the light shines, the darker shadows, and colour.

Touching: Feel the smoothness of the glass, and the stem. Is there any difference in texture or temperature? Perhaps close your eyes to enhance your sense of touch and explore the feel of the glass between your fingers, exploring its texture, weight and tactile sensations.

Smelling: Take a deep, full breath, and let it out. Slowly bring the glass up to your nose, and breathe in fully. With each inhalation drink in any aroma, or fragrance that may arise, noticing as you do this anything interesting that may be happening in your mouth or stomach. What smells can you detect? Is it peppery, grassy, fruity, astringent, buttery[1]?

Tasting: Now slowly bring the glass up to your lips, and gently breathe in, and then take a full sip of wine and hold it in your mouth without swallowing. Explore the sensations of it in your mouth, swirling it around. Focus on the felt experience. Is the wine smooth, or acid or even tasteless? Notice what happens in the aftermath, experiencing any waves of taste as you continue swirling it in your mouth. Notice how the taste changes as the wine warms in the mouth, and how this changes over time, and moment by moment

Swallowing: When you are ready, prepare to swallow the wine, and see if you can first detect the intention to swallow. Then, very consciously, swallow the mouthful, and notice what happens in the aftermath, any waves of taste that emanate from it. After swallowing, notice the remaining sensations of taste and texture in the mouth and, as well as any changes in the object itself.

Following: Feel what is left of the wine moving down into your stomach? Experience the sensations of drinking the wine, including any of light-headedness. Pay attention to how your body feels after drinking. This may highlight that drinking may not make you feel good. Finally, sense how the body as a whole is feeling afterwards.

CHAPTER 5 – OVERVIEW OF HABIT FORMATION AND HABIT BREAKING TECHNIQUES

> "Our character is basically a composite of our habits.
> Because they are consistent, often unconscious patterns,
> they constantly, daily, express our character."
> **Stephen Covey**

First, I'm going to discuss the principles of habit formation and breaking habits. Then I'm going to talk about a popular idea, that you only need 21 days (or 3 weeks) to break a habit, and finish with the idea of using triggers to break habits.

Of course, as we have shown in previous chapters, in reality, habits are complex and scientists still have a lot to learn about how they are formed, and in which parts of the brain. But in knowing this sort of stuff, we can put scientific knowledge to practical use, in habit breaking and forming techniques.

I'm going to use some of the learnings from the research in the previous chapters to talk about how to break a bad habit, using my own bad habit of drinking every day as an example. Of note, although this book is about breaking the bad habit of drinking, the techniques can be used to break **other bad habits**, and also to **form good habits**.

To repeat, the underlying principle of habit breaking (and habit forming) is repeated practicing of an action, until it becomes habitual. This process generally occurs in five stages[73]: awareness, intention, action, repetition, and consistent context.

FIVE STEPS TO BREAKING A BAD HABIT

One, awareness. I used to come home and have a wine---or two or three, especially if it had been a stressful day at work. Sometimes over the weekend, I'd have a couple of beers at lunch, then another beer and a couple of glasses of wine in the evenings. I found that every day, around lunch time, I'd start to anticipate having my daily glass/es of wine after work. Now, as I covered in the first couple of chapters, there is nothing wrong with **moderate** drinking, in fact, it can be quite good for you.

However, the safe limit for drinking is much less than most people realise. Women, for example, should have no more than 2 alcohol units per day, and no more than 14 per week. An alcohol unit is one mid strength beer (375mm) or 100ml of wine (approximately 1/3 of a normal red wine glass).

But over time (quite a lot of time, I was *very* resistant to change) I became aware that I drank quite a bit more than many of my friends, and much quicker too. For years, I justified this, even bragging about being able to 'drink anyone under the table', and telling scurrilous stories of my misspent youth: doing things like skinning dipping in a porthole pool over a bar for a dare---the dare being a six pack of beer; driving 18 hours cross country only stopping to buy beer or pee out the beer; or drinking so much that I passed out only to wake up on a float in the middle of a parade.

But as I got older, and started (horrors) peri-menopause, I began to realise that my drinking wasn't all that cool after all, and that if I thought about it, I didn't really respect those of my friends who drank to excess. Also, I am a frightful hypochondriac, and heavy drinking is linked to all sorts of nasty illnesses, of which I am terrified. My tolerance for alcohol was also getting worse, and it was starting to affect my digestion and in particular, my sleep---and I am rather fond of sleeping.

Two, intention. So I realised that my level of drinking was unhealthy, and that it was also habitual. I had tried to cut down previously, doing things like Moderation Management[74], Dry July and FebFast, but even if I managed a whole month, I would soon start drinking again. So I made a decision to quit drinking completely. Now, when I had given up drinking before, after about 3 days, I didn't really want anything to drink, and all the cravings went, so I knew that my drinking was more habitual than addiction.

So I had to plan how to break this habit, and more important, how to maintain the behaviour (not drinking). As we saw, in habit formation, they often start with a situational cue; a regular type of activity such as coming home after work, or meeting friends at the pub. Therefore, to break habits, it's important to break that link. If I always had a beer as soon as I came home, I found it useful to break that habit with a good habit.

Of note, it's important that the replacement habit be pleasurable (but not too pleasurable, or it could end up as a bad habit in itself, like substituting chocolate for drinking). Some replacement habits could be a few yoga poses, a nice walk, listening to a favourite song or having a nice hot bath.

I tried all of those, and found particularly, that if I did something, even if only for ten minutes or so, the craving would subside. You might have to do as I did, and avoid foods that normally go with alcohol---like cheese or nuts!

Three, action. Now, as I discussed earlier, there is often a vast gap between intention and actual behaviour. I normally find it easy not to drink on the first day of giving up---particularly as I tend to give up when I have a terrible hangover. Still, a couple of days in, I start to crave a drink as for me, every day had become a deeply engrained habit, and I was probably both psychologically and physically addicted to alcohol. So, I'd not drink for the week, then when weekend came around, I'd look for excuses to have a drink, or maybe just have a beer---which then led to 'just' having a glass (or two) of wine. It didn't help when I wasn't living alone, and my partner would drink, and ask if I wanted one---and I was *very* easily persuaded.

It usually went something like this, *"would you like a beer?"*

"No thanks, you know I'm not drinking."

"Are you sure, just one won't hurt?"

"Oh, all right".

Then I would have a beer, then persuade him to go and buy a bottle of wine, then I'd have two glasses of wine, and feel rather lightheaded from having not drunk the previous days, and have a hangover the next morning. Then I'd feel bad about myself, and stressed, and would have another glass or two of wine the next evening. By the next week of course, I was back to my normal drinking habits.

Four, repetition. Obviously I lapsed in my intentions to give up alcohol, but it is important to realise that lapses should not mean the end of your goal. It is **very important** to understand that lapses DO happen, and happen often, so you must not beat yourself up about them. One way in which this can be done is called coping planning, and is part of action. For example, I could write down the situations where I was mostly likely to want to drink, when I was feeling the most vulnerable, and thus more likely to lapse. I also tried planning for future events, say a work function where alcohol would be flowing freely, and volunteer to be the designated driver, so my abstinence was socially acceptable. I have also been to many social occasions where I just drank non-alcoholic drinks, but until they start serving non-alcoholic beer or wine, there is usually very little choice at functions---especially if don't like soft drinks.

The important thing is, to realise that temptation will be greater in certain circumstances, and make an action plan to deal with this. If you think that you truly cannot avoid drinking however, you may also choose to miss the event completely. That is easy for me, as I am quite antisocial, and hate going out at night, and I find it relatively easy not to drink at social events; my temptation unfortunately comes at home.

Five, consistent context. I also wanted to maintain my non-drinking over time, and in the same context. One way this can be done with drinking is to become known as a non-drinker, because consistency is also supported by the normal desire to be accepted by other humans. If I behave in a consistent manner (i.e. by not drinking on social occasions), then when or if I lapse, then people I know and work with will no doubt comment on the lapse, possibly in a negative manner. Most people don't like others pointing out the inconsistencies between what they say and what they do, so this is a very strong motivator---though it could lead to secret drinking for the seriously addicted. Human behaviour is very influenced by social and moral norms, and if your norm is not to drink, people *will* notice and comment if you do drink. Also, I've noticed that many people, even those who drink quite heavily and try and persuade you to join them, secretly (or not so secretly) respect you for not drinking, and lose a bit of this when you start again.

As my drinking habit was more related to night-time drinking at home, I also replaced this with another activity, performed at the same time. It is important to find something that is enjoyable. It is not much point trying to replace a habit with something you hate. What I did was try and remember hobbies that I enjoyed at other times, like crocheting or other craft work (pity that writing is not so enjoyable, I would have written heaps more books). You might like to go dancing, or paint, or sing or anything really. If lucky, you could discover an entirely new passion, and even take it up as a career, finding that drinking was related more to boredom and general life dissatisfaction, rather than addiction to alcohol. I sometimes play computer games, particularly Sudoku---though I have to be careful, as I find these are also addictive!

FIVE STAGES OF HABIT FORMATION

I'm going to use some of the learnings from the research in the previous chapters to talk about how to form a good habit, with examples. Although this book is about breaking the bad habit of drinking, the techniques can be used to break **other bad habits**, and to **form good habits**.

To repeat, the underlying principle of habit formation is repeated practicing of an action, until it becomes habitual. This process generally occurs in five stages[75]: awareness, intention, action, repetition, and consistent context.

First, awareness. Through a variety of cognitive and emotive processes, a person becomes **aware** of behaviour that they wish to practice more often or to change, in other words, to create or break a habit.

One of my ex-husbands (don't ask), let's call him Arthur (Art), used to be really good at sport; he was captain of the cricket team and was selected for the State team in the 400m sprint. However, since he left university, he did very little exercise. He's unfit, can't walk up hills without puffing, and his friends mocked his growing 'keg' (beer belly). One day at the pub, he met up with Steve, an old friend and fellow team mate from university, who'd recently moved back to the local area. Steve (despite being at the pub) was looking fantastic. He was really fit, and told Art all about his fitness regime, and how he just finished an ironman triathlon (42km run, 3.8km swim and 180km bike ride). Then he asked Art what sport he had done since graduating, and Art had to sheepishly admit, 'um, nothing'.

Art came home embarrassed at how he looked in comparison to Steve---especially as Art had been a *better* athlete than him; and terrified, as Steve had persuaded him to join him in his training sessions. Art was terrified that he would a) look like an idiot (he had claimed to be naturally fit) and b) of dying!

Second, intention. It's necessary to make the decision to take action. Prior to performing an actual non-habitual behaviour, a person goes through a psychological process called **intention**. However, as a multitude of studies have shown, the *intention to behave* does not necessary correspond with actual behaviour. New Year's resolutions are a perfect example of this. The relative influence of intention on behaviour (i.e. how likely it's that a person will carry out an intended behaviour) depends on how often they practice that behaviour[76].

If behaviour is regularly and frequently practiced – in other words, is habitual past behaviour – then that is a better predictor whether someone will carry out that behaviour. If you have been a jogger for many years, it's highly likely that you will continue to jog, unless you are injured, and even then you are likely to start again, or if not possible, take up another sport. If you have been a couch potato all your life, it is less likely that you will suddenly take up jogging---and if you do, it is also likely that you will give up jogging.

On the other hand, intentions are a better predictor for behaviours that are not frequent – in other words, not habitual. For example, choosing to cut automobile use if you rarely drive, is relatively well predicted by intention, but if you always drive, it's far more likely that you will continue to do so---unless you work very hard to break the habit.

One way that this can be beaten is by **planning**. An effective way of planning is to make implementation intentions; these are in the form of, 'when X happens, I will do Y', i.e. when I get home, I will go for a run.

After Art had impulsively agreed to train with Steve, he got a brief respite. When they met up again the next week, Steve said that he was going surfing in Bali for the next month and then was going to work for Engineers without Borders in Cambodia for two months. He said, when he came back, he'd contact Art, and they could go on some runs or bike rides.

Now Art felt even worse. He'd been given three months grace *but* he felt terrible because of how unfit he was, but also because he thought Steve was not only good looking and fit, but had an awesome life. For all he knew, he probably had a supermodel girlfriend too! Art's competitive nature was now triggered, so he made the decision to start training, so that when Steve got back, he wouldn't be completely useless or even drop dead of a heart attack in mid interval sprints.

To work on his fitness, Art had to make some plans. At the time, he was the co-owner of a franchise mechanical workshop, so he didn't have much time to spare. He had to plan his runs either in the early morning or early evening. I am a long time runner, but he wasn't interested in running with me (perhaps something to do with my running at 5am) and helped him research running routes, techniques for getting fitter and healthier eating habits. Not being a morning person, Art also decided to run in the evenings!

Three, **action**. The intention to behave must be translated into **action**. This is often the area where most good intentions fall by the wayside. No matter how good a person's intentions, many never do anything about these. This is a well-known psychological phenomenon called the 'attitude behaviour gap'. There are many reasons why intentions do not translate into actual behaviour, some of which are due to external circumstances, and some of which are due to psychological reasons.

External circumstances can also prevent many positive behaviours; for example, you might intend to ride your bike to work to save on fuel and also to get fitter, but when you wake up, it's raining, so you drive (just like every other day) and then you forget about your intention until the next time you puff and pant walking up the stairs. Or you might be concerned about global warming, and want to use solar power instead of electricity from coal-fired power plants. However, if you live in a rented flat, there is very little that you can do about getting solar power, so you just stick with the status quo.

The next night, Art came home from work (together with some brand new and expensive trainers and running shorts). He decided to go for a run around the block (around 2km). After 5 minutes, he was exhausted, and had to stop!

BREAKING THE BOOZE HABIT

He felt like an elephant was sitting on his chest. He had no worries about being hit by a car either, as his face was glowing bright red. He felt like he was going to both vomit and faint at the same time. Sweat poured down his body, and even worse, his chest and stomach were wobbling like jelly. His death was surely imminent---and if not, he was seriously considering a sports bra.

The next day I had to listen to hours of man-whinging; to hear the complaints, you would have thought he'd run the Comrades (Ultra) Marathon[77]. I had to even massage his calf muscles, while he constantly complained. Art literally wailed with the horror of having to run again---but what would happen when Steve returned? He *had* to. Oh the agony! Suffice it to say, as a 30 year running veteran, I was less than sympathetic.

Four, repetition. The desired habitual behaviour must be **repeated**. This usually requires motivation, as well as self-regulatory techniques, such as visual cues, diarising, vigilant control, community or family support.

One successful way to repeat desired behaviours is to join a group; where group support can help strengthen resolve to continue with the behaviour. This is the reason why organisations such as Weightwatchers and Alcoholics Anonymous can be so successful.

Unlike me, Art didn't like to run alone (well, at this stage, he didn't like to run, full stop), so I persuaded him to come along to Parkrun[78] which is a great community event, where people of all ages and abilities come together on a Saturday morning to go for a run (usually 5km). They encourage people of all ages and fitness levels and members often have runs at others times. Two days later, still feeling like he has been hit by a truck, Art went to Parkrun, where he meets other guys who are also trying to get fit.

After a few weeks of going to Parkrun, Art could run 5km without walking, even once, and without feeling as if he needs to go to the emergency ward. Even better, his clothes were becoming looser, especially around the waist. The support of the other guys in the club is really helpful, and there is an informal telephone tree, so that if anyone is slacking off, they get a telephone call, with encouragement to attend. After three months, Art finds that he has to go running at least twice a week, or else he started getting frustrated. He also found that he was sleeping much better at night, and had cut down on his drinking.

Five, **consistent context**. 'The new action must be repeated in a fashion conducive to the development of automaticity. Recent studies showed that participants encouraged to perform a health-promoting behaviour (e.g., eating fruit, drinking water, taking physical activity) regularly in consistent contexts reported increases in habit-related automaticity'[79].

What does this mean? I'll describe what it means in the context of Art's fitness regime.

Art sets himself a routine for his running by attending Parkrun once a week, and going for runs with his new running buddies another couple of days a week. He thus performed the behaviour regularly (every second day) and in consistent contexts (either directly after work, or at the running club). Importantly, he also receives positive feedback because he feels better, has lost weight, and enjoys the friendship of the other people at the running club. Art is rapidly beginning to make running part of his life, and although he's still afraid of training with Steve, is far more confident than 3 months ago.

As we can see, above are some techniques that people can use to make or break habits. But how long do you have to practice these behaviours until the habit is formed or goes away? Is there any truth to the idea of the rule of three?

The rule of three

There is a popular saying or 'rule of thumb' that it takes 3 days for a 'craving' to go away, 3 weeks to get used to something, and 3 months to make it habit. But is this true, and is it based on the actual science of habit formation[80]?

As shown in the previous chapters, habits are patterns of behaviour that become paths worn across the lawn of our brains ('neurons that fire together, wire together'). If you do the same thing at the same time every day, like wake up, turn on the radio and then go to the kitchen to make yourself some coffee, then get up and go for a run or walk (which, incidentally is exactly what I do every morning, and to which my dog is also habituated), then these actions, and the cues for them, have established a synaptic pathway in your brain.

Say you go for a hike through a national park. The park managers have constructed a trail that zigzags up and down a steep slope, to prevent against erosion, and also to make climbing the hill easier for some. However, many people take shortcuts and instead of zigzagging, they cut straight up the hill between the zigs and the zags. In time, the alternate path becomes deeper and more worn, particularly if it's not too precipitous. The more the shortcut becomes used, the more people use it, so it becomes difficult to differentiate between the proper trail, and the 'easier' trail that people have created.

That is essentially what habits are, shortcuts through the neural pathways of the brain. The brain gets so used to taking the shortcut, and the more that it's used, the deeper it becomes, and the easier it's to carry out those actions. Thus, a habit's formed, where the actions and the cues for the actions become almost instinctive and unconscious.

So, how do you rewire the brain to think in different ways? How do you get rid of the habitual path, the one that is leading to soil erosion and damaging sensitive vegetation? How do you get the vegetation to grow over the shortcut, so that people are forced to use the correct path?

Now, unfortunately, as we have shown before, forming bad habits is normally a lot easier than getting rid of bad habits, or for that matter, forming new good habits. No matter how many times the park rangers close off the shortcut track, or put up signs saying that it's a revegetation area, someone is bound to push aside or jump over the barrier.

So, what about the rule of three? Is it scientific? Can we really use it to break a habit or create a new habit? The idea that the rule of three helped with habits originated, like many of these things, in a self-help book, in this case one called Psycho-Cybernetics, which was published in the 1970s.

The concepts in this book were then taken up in the Readers Digest (the pre-internet method of something going viral; I feel unbelievably ancient, as I got much of my childhood information from the Readers Digest).

The idea of three subsequently became part of popular 'knowledge' and variations have been oft repeated in many popular self-help or pop psychology books since, including the multi-million dollar bestseller, The Secret (which said that 30 days were needed to break a habit).

As with any popular self-help ideas, this idea contains a kernel of truth. Researchers have found that it takes approximately 66 days (rounded up to say, 10 weeks) to create a new habit[81][82]. If you bodge this, maybe close one eye, and wish really hard, that could be assumed to be round about 12 weeks, or three months (pity science doesn't really work like that, it tends to rely on more accurate estimations than a 10% error on either side).

However, if the rule of three, 30 days or whatever duration that some self-help author has invented were true---no-one ever made any money telling people that it will take months if not years to change, even though that is generally true---it would be relatively easy to break habits. However, it's perfectly obvious, just by looking around, that people cling to their bad habits. Despite all the self-help books, people are still overweight, smoke, don't exercise, watch too much TV, eat too much junk food and drink too much.

Also, people are different. For some, it may well only take 21 days to break a habit, for others, it might take 21 months, or even years, or never. This depends on the person concerned, how long they have had the habit, whether the habit's physically as well as psychologically addictive, who they associate with, and a million other variables that are unique to a particular person.

No, unfortunately, breaking habits is not as easy as not doing something for 3 days, or 21 days, or 3 months. The synaptic pathways that have been worn into your brain are there forever, particularly if you have had the habit for many years. It's like moving into an old house, and finding a groove in the floorboards from a chair that sat in the same place for 50 years. There is no way that that groove is ever going to go away unless you replace the entire floor.

Breaking habits can be done however---or I wouldn't need to write this book---and I will discuss how to use my technique to do so, but it does require constant attention and vigilant control---but if you replace the bad habit with a good habit, if you create a new, paved path between your house and the shed, in time, the old path might become more faded and overgrown, so you are less likely to want to use it anymore.

False memories

Another way in which we can break bad habits is to set up false memories. What on earth do I mean by this? Well, some recent research has showed that when subjects were given false memories about food that made them sick as a child (which weren't true) they tended to eat less of that food[83].

Now apart from the obvious concern that we should have about how easy it is to set up a false memory, and how little we should trust our own memories and experience, we CAN use this technique to help break habits. How?

Well, if you are reading this, you probably want to give up or cut down on your drinking. To use the false memory technique, you might repeatedly tell yourself about times when you got sick after drinking a certain amount or type of alcohol. Then in future, you might avoid that drink entirely.

I recently had to put this into practice, not with a false memory, but with real life experience. I have developed an intolerance to alcohol, and its effects have made me feel really ill, even with only a small amount to drink (2 glasses of wine). If I drank wine, it gave me horrible side effects, such as sweating, nausea, sinus and worst of all, palpitations. The most recent time I gave up alcohol in August 2016, I woke up with such a racing heart, that I thought I was having a heart attack. I already suffer from health anxiety (which, by the way, is the subject of my next book), so this was not very reassuring. I had to use all my relaxation techniques not to go into a full blown panic attack (which are horrible).

Because I remember how awful and afraid I felt that last time I drank, I then gave up alcohol for 5 months. Now I am not 100% certain that it was the alcohol that caused this, it could have just been a panic attack (I am an anxious person), but the mere thought of that has been enough to make me swear off alcohol. I started drinking again, but soon realised that I am not currently able to limit my drinking to only one glass of wine, so I have now given up again.

I can drink other alcohol in moderation, but I love wine, so I just choose not to drink at all; especially as, unlike non-alcoholic wine, which tastes quite revolting and is only improved by adding real wine; non-alcoholic beer is very nice, and you can drink it any time without feeling guilty.

BREAKING THE BOOZE HABIT

You can create false memories[84] in yourself (or others, but I strongly suggest that you limit this to yourself---doing it to others may have nasty repercussions[85]) by various methods.

> Think of something that you want to give up. Only use it for something you **really** want to give up, that is bad for you, such as drinking too much, smoking, eating too much junk food or sugar etc. For this example, let's say that you want to give up drinking.
>
> Tell yourself a story about how it made you feel really bad---it's probably quite easy to do if you drink a lot, as you don't have to imagine anything, just remember a horrible hangover or embarrassing episode. Try to imagine the episode as if it really occurred, how you felt emotionally, what were the sounds and smells and sights around you at the time, and what other people were saying. Childhood or early memories are particularly good for this. Tell yourself a story, or recall a true memory about how you got really sick after drinking a specific drink, such as Tequila.
>
> Tell your story to your friends and family or share it on Facebook. You might find that some of your family even profess to remember the episode (or actually **do** remember it). The more lurid the story, the better. Disgusting side effects like diarrhea and vomiting, especially in public, should give the story that ring of authenticity. Cider, for instance, gives me an instant upset stomach, and I still feel guilty about the time that I had to duck behind an ornate building on a busy Cape Town street, and use a pile of cardboard boxes as an emergency toilet stop.
>
> 4Finally, repeat the story to yourself whenever you think about the subject or you are tempted to have some alcohol. Just imagine embarrassing yourself in public because of drinking too much. (Sadly, I had a very misspent youth, between about 18 and 24, and don't have to imagine anything---I just have to remember things).

Now this may not work for everyone, but if it doesn't work for you, well, you may have triggered some of your creative side, and decide to take up writing or another creative pursuit---because this is what writers do every day.

Using Triggers to Break Habits

I'm using triggers instead of the word 'cues' as used in the section about how habits are formed. This is deliberate, as the meaning of what I want to convey is subtly different. By *cue*, I mean the definition 'a stimulus, either consciously or unconsciously perceived, that elicits or signals a type of behaviour'; and a *trigger* is something that initiates a reaction, or chain of events.

BREAKING THE BOOZE HABIT

A cue is as complex series of events, and a trigger as a simple, single event or action.

We have seen how habits are formed when behaviours are frequently repeated, in a consistent manner, usually in the presence of specific cues. Having a beer in your local pub might provide the cues to light up a cigarette. This is because that behaviour is practiced in the same context repeatedly, and the brain doesn't like to have to give over too much of its processing power to familiar behaviours. Just as cyclists often cut corners on badly designed bike paths, the brain also likes to take short cuts, to save effort and time.

Remove yourself from the cues

One way to break habits is to remove yourself from the cues that led to the formation of the habit in the first place. If on your way home from work, you habitually stop in at the pub, take a different route. If you find yourself lighting up a cigarette whilst watching the evening news, do something else at the same time. If you have to move house, try and find a new place that will give you the opportunity to cycle or ride to work instead of driving.

When I was about 23, I decided to give up smoking. I identified that the most common times that I smoked were when I was out socially, having a drink with friends. But every time I had a beer, I wanted a cigarette. So, I also had to give up drinking.

A relatively easy (or very difficult, depending on how much change you like) way to change your behaviour is work with other changes in your life, such as changing jobs or moving house. My choice not to go out and drink with my friends, was made easier when I moved back home, as my parents lived on a farm 50km from the nearest town. If I wanted to go out, I had to drive 50km, and then I couldn't drink as I had to drive home, and didn't want to lose my license or have an accident. Also, I hate driving, especially at night.

Another way you might achieve this is by piggybacking on something like a new relationship (say your new partner does not like smoking, or does not drink much) or if you intend to go travelling, and it's more convenient not to have to look for cigarettes or alcohol, particularly in countries where smoking or drinking is not commonplace. If you want to give up drinking, what about going on a physically active holiday (although I have been known to take entire bottles of wine on 5 day hikes) or travel to an Islamic country, where drinking is not socially unacceptable. You might find that the brief break in your routine is enough to give you a great start. Then, feeling healthier will give you the intrinsic incentive to continue.

BREAKING THE BOOZE HABIT

Use triggers or reminders

However, not everyone can move house, dump their partner or go on an overseas holiday just to change a habit, and perhaps taking a different route when driving home will add half an hour on to your commute.

So a less extreme method is to **slightly** change your environment by placing reminders or *triggers*. For example, studies have shown that placing attractive recycling bins next to the ordinary garbage bins, encourages people to recycle more; or placing notices next to the elevator, that encourage people to take the stairs, have also been successful in getting more people to walk.

If you wish to start a habit of running every day---although if you have not run in decades, I suggest first getting a medical check, and beginning with walk/running---this requires a number of different actions, as well as context. So you might choose to habituate a simpler action related to the running, such as putting on your running shoes or putting your socks and shoes by the front door before you go to bed.

If you wish to break a complex habit, such as drinking wine or snacking after meals, you might concentrate on another simpler trigger, such as brushing your teeth. Once you have brushed your teeth, this can be a trigger that tells you that no more food or drink is going to be taken that night, as you are preparing for bed. I put my dog out every night to do her business, and she knows that's the trigger for going to bed (and sometimes, a late night snack).

Another method is to place visual triggers in places where you see them every day. If you want to start a habit to floss your teeth every night and the dental floss is in the cupboard under the sink, behind piles of old makeup and empty shampoo bottles to get at it, you are likely to forget to floss (gym syndrome, it's inconvenient, so you don't bother). But if you put the floss on top of the sink, next to your toothbrush, then you are much more likely to remember to floss.

For example, one young writer used his compulsory password changes to change his life[86]. Many of you might work in the type of office that requires you to change your password once a month or so. Almost everyone has passwords on their personal PC, mobile telephone or tablet; and of course, on your social media pages, internet banking, and so on.

The writer had just suffered a breakup and was going through the usual pain, anger and grief that accompanies a major life challenge such as the breakup of a relationship. He told of how he was forced to change his password, and as is typical, to use capital letters, numerals etc. When he changed his password, he changed it to 'Forgive@h3r".

83

Then, every time his computer went into energy saving mode or when he logged on in the mornings, he had to type in that password. He spoke of how every time he typed that phrase, he thought about what he was writing (thus, he used also used mindfulness techniques), his anger lessened, and moreover, he became less depressed. He spoke of how in less than a month, he had little or no anger against his ex-wife.

The next time he had to change his password, he used the phrase 'Quit@smoking4ever'. He said that literally the next day, he quit smoking, and to this day, has not smoked a cigarette. All of his password changes worked, except for one which said 'Eat2times@day' worked. I'm not sure why that one did not work, perhaps his work was boring, and he ate out of boredom, perhaps he has low blood sugar and needed food more often. Still, this is a really easy technique for people to try---but of course, don't publish your passwords online, or tell anyone what they are, or you may end up losing more than weight.

I've done this myself, such when I first gave up drinking for the month of July (Dry July as it's known here) last year, and it does work to help you become more conscious of your goals. I changed my work password to nodrinkingB4Aug (it was only on my work computer, so don't try and hack it; all you will get is boring research articles, which you can get for free anyway).

Recently, I thought I was spending too much time on social media, so I changed my password to a quote from my favourite poet, Mary Oliver, and interspersed it with various characters, numbers and different capital letters. I also changed all my settings to forget my password and not automatically fill it in when I login. Now I have to type this in every time I want to go on Facebook. It works wonders, as it is such a pain to remember and type it correctly!

If you create visual triggers for each time you practice (or don't practice) a habit, then this can reinforce your behaviour, and to remind you to practice the new habit. My visual trigger not to drink, which I will detail in the following sections, is to have a system of stars, which I then stick on a calendar, which is in my bedroom, and which I have habituated myself to doing every day.

CHAPTER SIX: LET'S PUT IT ALL TOGETHER---THE TECHNIQUE

> "Your net worth to the world is usually determined by what remains after your bad habits are subtracted from your good ones". **Benjamin Franklin**

INTRODUCTION

So, you have an issue---or like me, you have many issues. You may be quite happy with some of these (others may not be happy with them, but that is their problem, isn't it) or you may want to change some or all of them.

So, what do you do? The first thing people do is to identify the problem. That is usually quite easy. Almost everyone knows something about themselves that they want to change. They also know things about *other people* that they want to change, but this is a self-help book, not a do-it-yourself divorce manual. This book is about cutting down or giving up alcohol, so this is the habit to which I will dedicate the most time, but it can also be used for other habits.

This technique works. I've used it successfully to break two bad habits (drinking too much wine, and snacking after dinner) and to start one good habit, finishing this book. Every year since I was about ten (I was one of those horrid precocious children, for which I got bullied unmercifully) I made a goal that I was going to write a book. As I got older, I made this goal every year. By the time I get to 30, I shall have published a book. By the time I get to 40, I shall have published a book. By the time I get to 50, I will publish a book.

But have I published any books (journal articles don't count)? Nope. I start each book, motivated---write a bit, then get bored and do other stuff. If I ever become a famous writer (lol), there will be an awful lot of work for my future biographers. To be honest, I did write three (very bad) fiction books. Mercifully no-one wanted to publish them, particularly as my plotting skills are like my musical ability, which is zero. But where would musicians be without listeners?

BREAKING THE BOOZE HABIT

> **Hints**
>
> - Take small steps. Don't try to do everything at once. (So, instead of "I'm going to give up drinking cold turkey" start with "I'm going to have at least two days every week without drinking any alcohol", or "I'm going to drink no more than 14 alcohol units in any week, and no more than a maximum of 4 in one day")
> - Only change one habit at a time. Instead of saying, 'I'm going to cut down my drinking, start exercising, and quit smoking', start with cutting down drinking.
> - Write down the habit you want to change, and write down specific sub-goals for achieving the broader. The brain doesn't like fuzzy future goals, it prefers to break these down into manageable tasks so your big goal may not seem so daunting.
>   - For example, rather than writing 'I will exercise,' write, 'I will start walking 30 minutes twice a week, on Monday and Thursday, and I will wake up at 7 a.m., so I can walk before work on those days.')
> - Repeat the desired behaviour as often as you can. The more you repeat a behaviour, the more likely it becomes 'instinctive.'[1]

Ok, so let's first get into breaking a bad habit. Initially, we need to identify what habit we want to break and understand why it is a habit.

Identify the habit you want to break and why it's a habit

Journaling

Linda was constantly losing and regaining the same 5kg. She'd procrastinate for months, and then make a decision to lose 5kg, usually as a result of an upcoming wedding or school reunion. She tried every diet and weight-loss technique on the market. Many were successful---in the short term.

The majority of diets work in the short term because they reduce your food intake. Whether you choose a healthy, balanced diet, or an unscientific fad diet like the cabbage soup or blood type diet, you *will lose weight* if you stick to it. Who on earth can eat 2000 calories of cabbage soup a day? Also, you wouldn't very pleasant to be around, let's hope you don't work in an enclosed space.

Anyway, as soon as Linda reached her goal weight, she'd revert back to her old habits. Sooner or later, she would end up back where she started.

Linda did this for many years, and managed to keep at more or less the same weight---until she reached her mid-40s. Suddenly, she no longer found it so easy to lose weight, and she had learned some very bad food habits over the years. Now, to lose the weight, she had to cut her food down to much smaller portions, and do far more exercise. This really frustrated her, especially when she noticed that she was putting on weight in different places. When she was younger, she used to put weight on her hips and bum. Now she was putting on weight around her stomach. Her once flat stomach (even when she was 'fat') was now flabby, and no amount of crunches and sit-ups made any difference.

And her weight began trending upwards. In her 20s, her normal weight was around 58kg, in her 30s, around 62kg, and now it was around 65kg. Worst of all, when she joined a new gym, her body fat percentage was way up, now nearly 30% fat, even though her actual weight and height were normal for her age.

Linda decided that this could not continue or she would be a fat old lady, but how could she permanently change her habits?

But what exactly was the habit that Linda wanted to break? Was it eating too much? Was it eating the wrong foods? Was it eating at the wrong time? Eating as comfort, as stress relief, out of boredom?

If you want to change your behaviour, you have to first understand the behaviour that you want to change, and what influences this behaviour.

Linda began to use a simple technique to identify her eating behaviour. **She started a food diary**, and at the same time, wrote down how she was feeling when she ate. Naturally, there is an app (or lots of apps) that can do this for you. I recommend MyFitnessPal[87]

YOUR journal

If your problem is habitual drinking, smoking, gambling or anything else, you can do the same thing. Make a note each time you perform the behaviour that you wish to modify, what time you do it, what you are doing at the time, and how you are feeling. You could write "Got home at 5.30pm, stressed, had a glass of wine while cooking dinner". Of course, this would probably read more like, "effing horrible day, need wine NOW, before I kill someone."

The purpose of this is not to work out how many calories you are eating, how many drinks you have (although that is useful information), or how much money you spend on internet shopping. It's to identify patterns of behaviour.

At this time, you are NOT trying to change anything, you are just journaling.

This exercise does not have to be difficult or time consuming, and only needs to take, at the most, around five minutes a day, or half an hour a week.

BREAKING THE BOOZE HABIT

You could use one of the templates (in the Appendices) or create your own Excel or Word table, such as the one on the next page, which gives an example of what you might do to quit drinking. The last column, awareness of action, is an indication of how much you were aware of performing the habit.

It's quite scary when you write down what you actually eat or drink; when you realise that you drink way more than you think you do (or have persuaded yourself that you do). With food, it is really scary when you weigh your portions and see how little a recommended serving such as 100g of wonderful food (i.e. cheese) actually is. I use an app called MyFitnessPal[88], which has a huge database of food (including non US food), and you can also scan the barcode on packaged food, to get all the nutrient information immediately. Bear in mind however, that most people are horrendously bad at accurately estimating quantities of food[89], not to mention are horrendous liars and often discount food eaten while tasting other food; so you need to be ruthlessly honest with everything you put in your mouth---ok, maybe not *everything*---and you really do need a good kitchen scale.

Analysis

After doing this for a week, it's important to analyse the information (the Appendices give you further information on how to go about doing this).

Things to look out for are:

> - **Consistent settings:** where is the most common place you practice the habit;
> - **Consistent feelings:** do you have any consistent feelings during the habit, like boredom, irritation or worry; and
> - **Lack of awareness;** this is the hardest---keep a lookout for times that you do things without thinking, like snacking.

This is going to be a bit of a pain but it's for a relatively short period of time, and will give you some valuable insight into your behaviour---and you only have to do it once.

Also, try and do this activity in a typical week. It's not much point doing it in weeks when you are really stressed, or in different environments, such as on vacation, or during holiday times like Christmas or Easter, or if you have particularly tedious relatives visiting.

If you absolutely cannot do this for a week, try and do it for as long as you can, around a minimum of three days should be ok.

BREAKING THE BOOZE HABIT

How I finally gave up drinking

When I wanted to give up drinking, I started a drinking journal, before I did anything else. Eventually, I carried on doing a briefer version of the journal as part of the calendar technique (next section).

As you can see, it is easy to drink quite a lot, without really being aware of it That is 6 AU (Alcohol Units) over the period of about 3 hours, which would put most women (and men) over the driving limit, and is also considered binge drinking. I know people who could easily drink that 3+ days a week, without considering themselves binge drinkers, and potentially damaging their health.

Table 1: Heather's Drinking Journal (weekday)

Time	Habit	Setting	Feelings (i.e. sad, bored, happy)	Aware (1-5)
17h00	1 beer (375ml) 1 AU	Kitchen	Just got home after work. Stressed out because of the traffic and irritated because got nothing effective done at work	2
17h30	1 wine (200ml) 2AU	Deck	Slightly stressed, feeling better after the beer. First glass of wine tastes so nice. Relaxed	4
18h30	1 wine (200ml) 2AU	Kitchen	Felt like a second glass, cooking dinner for the family, doesn't taste as nice as the first. So-so, makes cooking dinner easier.	1
19h30	I wine (100ml) 1AU	Lounge	During dinner, have to help husband with a spreadsheet for work and don't feel like it. He doesn't offer to wash up either. Tired and irritated.	3

Of course, there will be days when I forgot to write in the journal; like when I was more stressed, or work was giving me the sh*ts, or the husband was being more demanding than usual; so sometimes I'd have to do it a couple of days later and try and remember. But I did this for 2 weeks, and managed to complete at least 80% of the entries; even if some were a bit bodgy because I couldn't remember. It's also important to be honest. No-one is going to see this but you, so don't lie to yourself.

After I finished the journal, I looked at the patterns when I was most likely to drink. Because my day job is a data analyst, I graphed times, places and amount of drinks and even did little charts against my feelings at the time. Of course, most of you are probably not data nerds, so you could just read your journal and get a good inkling of when you are more likely to want a drink. **The important thing is to get an understanding of when you are more likely to drink without thinking about it---when it's completely habitual.**

The reason I did this was to **increase awareness**; as through a variety of cognitive and emotive processes, a person becomes aware of a type of behaviour that they wish to practice more often or to change, in other words, to create or break a habit.

After reading my journal, where I was more or less honest, I noticed that at certain times of day, I was used to having a beer, or a wine. I also tended to drink more wine if I drank beer first, and if I didn't drink between 5pm and 7pm, then I was likely not to drink at all. I also noticed that my drinking was habitual after having the first glass, I drank the second mostly without noticing what it tasted like or even enjoying it. Also, if I drank whilst cooking or watching TV, then I would drink mindlessly, and quite fast, not even noticing until I had finished the glass. And if the bottle was finished, then I wanted more. On the rare occasion I went out socially, I also drank without thinking, talking and drinking too much (if I wasn't the designated driver).

There were also patterns to when I drank, with different times are associated with completely different feelings. When I analysed a typical weekday I saw that when I got home from work, I had a beer both as a **reward** for getting over the **stress** of driving home in traffic and because I was **thirsty** from not drinking enough water during the day. I can actually drink beer without getting habituated, but it makes me feel instantly relaxed, and then want wine.

After the beer, which I drank really quickly, I would go on to the deck and have a large glass of wine, to **relax** before cooking dinner. I knew my husband would not be home for an hour or so, and I had at least half an hour to relax. I felt guilty, as I should have walked the dogs but I loved sitting on the deck drinking wine, and was strongly conditioned to want this every day. I felt really **good**, and was **aware** of the taste of the wine, and how quickly it **relaxed** me.

Near the end of the glass, I would often drink the wine faster than I should, which made me feel a bit **rushed** because I knew my husband would soon be home and want his dinner. I didn't mind cooking for him, he had a much more demanding job than me. I then would finish my wine a bit **too quickly** and went to the kitchen to start dinner, where I would pour another large glass. Despite the wine, I began to feel **less relaxed**, and somewhat **irritated**. I would rather have been sitting on the deck instead of slaving in the kitchen.

BREAKING THE BOOZE HABIT

Also, the second glass of wine tasted **less pleasant** than the first, and I tended to drink it rather **mindlessly** as I cooked, taking sips and **not really being aware** of drinking. In this way, I drank too fast, and felt rather tiddly.

On that day, when my husband came home, he was in a **bad mood** from work, and instead of saying hello, he just asked 'where's dinner?' This made me feel **stressed and irritated**. I had another glass of wine with dinner, and had to fight the **urge to argue** with him, as my inhibitions have been relaxed by the alcohol. I was also **tired** (from the wine and the stress). After dinner, I told my husband that I had a **bad headache** and went to bed, where I lay, feeling angry, but also a bit **dizzy and sick**. I fell asleep quickly but had a **bad night** from the wine, and in the morning, my husband complained that I had snored loudly all night. I vowed to give up drinking for the 4th time this month.

Through doing this exercise, I became more aware of two things:

1) *The times when I was more likely to drink without thinking, and*
2) *The personal rewards that I associated with drinking.*

Importantly, I was becoming aware of the regular settings and times when I drank (I think I am a slow learner). To break this habit, I needed to become *more aware* when and why I drank---as the Buddhists call it, mindfulness (as detailed in the previous chapter).

I also needed to break the link between drinking and rewards. This is because my drinking is not just about the addiction to alcohol, it's also about the **psychological addiction to the act, and to rewards associated with it.**

But we have learned that changing the reward is almost [90]impossible, so we need to change the behaviour yet still get the SAME reward.

So, how did I break the link?

I had the second aspect of the habit model; namely, intention (what was it, the 4th time I'd wanted to give up that month), but now I needed **take action** and first I had to **fully understand the rewards** that I got for drinking.

So what are my rewards?

I now had a much deeper insight into my behaviour, but I also needed to understand the rewards associated with it. To do this, I could use my own self-knowledge, or use some resources (like the quizzes in the Appendices).

For me, the afternoon beer was associated with relieving thirst and relieving **stress**. I could ask myself, '**what else** can I do to relieve thirst and stress'?

91

Well, obviously I could first drink something other than beer to relieve my thirst, as well as making sure that I drank enough during the day, by carrying a water bottle, or getting one of those cool 'smart water bottles' with a built in app that tells you when you have not had enough to drink[91]. What I actually did was buy NON alcoholic beer, and keep this cold in my fridge---it tasted the same, and quenched my thirst!

I could also **educate myself** that alcohol is NOT a stress reliever, but actually creates more stress on my body. There are many resources that can give someone a basic understanding of what happens to your body when you drink too much alcohol (see Chapter 2).

However, there's another psychological factor at play here, and that is called *cognitive dissonance*[92], which is basically the feeling of (more) stress that arises from holding conflicting beliefs. The brain tries really hard to reconcile behaviour with beliefs, and will frequently abandon beliefs to justify behaviour. Indeed, research has shown (sadly) that sometimes providing information to counter false beliefs only serves to harden those beliefs (the backfire effect)[93].

Another thing I could do would be to list some things that I enjoy doing, which I could do **instead of having a wine**. For example, I might have a cup of my favourite tea, or even a square of expensive chocolate (not too much, I didn't want to replace drinking with another habit like eating too much sugar), or I could take the dog for a run or a walk and enjoy the good feeling that comes from exercise, and the happiness at sharing the dog's joy in simple things. Exercise is wonderful to curb cravings, as the blood flowing through your body makes you far less likely to want to drink afterwards.

One thing I also did was to do some **self-analysis** and understand why I got so **irritated** cooking and cleaning for my husband. Was it because I **resented** that he **didn't appreciate me**; that I always had to do the cooking and cleaning as well as working full time? I could talk to him, and ask him to help out with **his share** of the chores, including cooking, or if he really was too busy, I could cook a week's worth of dinners on a day when I was less busy. I quite enjoy cooking really, but not the feeling that I *have* to cook.

What I also did was change my **attitude** to drinking. I recognized (using this, and also self-awareness and mindfulness techniques) that my drinking is not necessarily a solution to my stressful life and that in the long run, it can make it worse (and definitely add to tension by making me less careful about what I said to my husband when I was irritated).

I also thought of people who didn't drink, and compared them with people who drank too much. Then I said, **who do I respect more**? Do I respect the habitual drinkers, or my 'heroes' who don't drink? I also looked at YouTube clips of drunk people, and asked myself, do I want to be like them?

What I also do is try and read a lot about what alcohol can do to my body, and how it is implicated in so many serious health problems (and I have health anxiety, particularly about cancer, and alcohol is linked to a number of cancers). Also, the more I read, the more aware I became about how much drinking could harm me, and the more it moved more to the forefront of my mind (**vigilant control**), so that my drinking could be less habitual, and I am more likely to not want to drink.

Finally, I researched how much drinking cost me every year, and this was quite terrifying. I was spending about $300 per month just on alcohol (including going out to pubs etc). That added up to $3,600 per year---equivalent to TWO international return flights to awesome places. That alone was good enough incentive not to drink anymore (and not to buy cheap alcohol instead, as I only like craft beer or good Shiraz anyway, lol).

Do you see what I mean? If you change your thinking, you can change your attitude.

But still, changing your attitude is not going to change your behaviour, particularly for something as physically and psychologically addictive as drinking. I had changed my attitude to drinking many times, and still drank.

So, what did I do next?

Change the context in which the habit occurs

As we showed in the previous chapters, **a habit is formed when behaviour is repeated in a stable context**. For example, you start a new job, and it's a little bit further away from home than your previous job. You used to ride your bicycle to work, but now it's just that little bit more inconvenient---and also, the ride to work is less pleasant, as instead of cycling through a park, you have to ride on a busy road or as I do now, down (and back up) a very steep hill WITH fast traffic.

So you begin driving to work instead. Every day now, you get in your car, and drive the same route to work. You have now established a new habit, to drive to work, at a certain time, by a certain route.

Now I used to drink in certain contexts, at home after I got back from work, on the deck and in the kitchen, and also at various social occasions over the weekend; and in response to certain cues. As people are all different (yes, really), these cues and contexts also differ.

For example, when I was in my late teens, I took up drinking, and I am going to describe to you about contexts and cues using these as examples.

BREAKING THE BOOZE HABIT

Drinking:

I had been at boarding school since the age of 9, where I had been bullied terribly; and I had recently moved countries to escape a war zone, and had grown up in a very isolated and remote area of Africa (I was like my rescue dog Princess---aka The Terrierist---insufficiently socialised). My father, who I doted on and desperately wanted to be the son that he never had (he had 3 daughters), was also typical of the 'English' style of never show your emotions, don't show weakness, and never ever hug or kiss anyone. Hence, I grew up un-socialised, unable to express emotions (also, at boarding school, they beat you up if you cried), yet very ambitious and with a million goals (which change daily).

By the time I was 16, I was a very attractive young woman, and clever at school, but also pathologically shy. Nonetheless, I was very interested in boys, but couldn't talk to them, without stammering and blushing bright red. My best friend and I had this rather bet (in retrospect), that we wouldn't leave school whilst still being virgins, and I was determined to beat her. At one party, I discovered the 'joys' of drinking as a cure for shyness.

Drinking cured my shyness, but it also released my formerly suppressed wild side (boarding school, bullies and strict parents will do that). Put it like this, when I was aged about 17, after that first party, about which I can recall very little, I gained the nickname (from the Chris de Burgh song) of Patricia the Stripper. Nearly 4 decades later, I can still remember all the words!

Now, it was normal to drink when going out, and all my friends drank, and it was cool. Also, my parents and family would criticise me for drinking and bad behaviour, which made me drink more, because I was a rebellious teenager. The more they criticised me, the more I rebelled, so it was a vicious circle.

We used to go out every night, go to 'ladies nights' where everyone would get horribly drunk and play party games, where the prizes of course, were alcohol. Then they would let the guys in around 10pm. I was very good at 'down-downs' (skulling beer) and would win 6-packs or bottles of wine, so I could drink free. On weekends, my sister and I would take our sleeping bags to a secluded beach, make ourselves a BBQ, and then sleep all day in a cave.

I then spent about 4 years partying, dropping out of various colleges, and started hanging around with rather a bad crowd, who were also into the old sex, drugs and rock and roll. I began modelling, but it was more like soft porn, with things like jumping naked out of cakes for sports teams or posing nude for magazine shoots. I wasn't really such a bad girl, just lonely and shy, but the more I used alcohol to cover up my basic self, the more I did stupid things, and the more I felt I had to justify these by rebelling even more.

I'm not sure whether there was a specific event that made me change, but I began to tire of this life, especially when I heard of friends and family getting degrees, settling down and doing other stuff that sounded much more interesting, like travelling the world. I remember thinking, when my one cousin got a degree, that 'I'm much cleverer than her, how come *she* got a degree!' I also felt sleazy and dirty, and always sick. Another trigger, was this was when the AIDS epidemic first began (in the early 80s) and being a hypochondriac, I was terrified of getting AIDS, which given the sex and drugs (and rock and roll, I once (briefly, before Daddy came to find me) ran off with Suzi Q's lead guitarist---ah misspent youth) certainly would have had quite a high probability.

So, I moved back to the farm where my parents lived, took up running, and although I didn't give up drinking, I cut down dramatically and I gave up smoking. I also made new friends, and turned my back on that old life. I'm just happy that I did all that stuff when I was young and stupid, and didn't get to middle-age thinking, 'what did I miss'? (Answer: nothing in particular, though will make an entertaining story should I ever write my memoirs).

Smoking:

The first time I tried smoking, at the relatively late age of 16, I had utterly no idea how to do it. I went behind the athletics stadium with my friend Jenna, who said to me, *'want to come for a smoke?'* I readily agreed. She handed me the cigarettes and the matches. I held the cigarette between my thumb and forefinger, as I'd seen others do, and tried to light it.

Jenna looked at me, "*have you ever smoked before?*" she demanded.

"*Oh yes, all the time*" I lied.

She was utterly unconvinced, rolled her eyes, took the cigarette away from me, lit it properly and then handed it back to me. I took a huge puff, and was completely incapacitated by coughing. Yeah right, I smoked all the time.

I smoked because mostly because it annoyed my non-smoking parents and because back then (in the late 70s) it was considered 'cool' and 'bad'. Every day after school, I had to wait half an hour for my bus. All of us 'bad' people used to hang around outside the shopping center which was opposite the bus stop. Bear in mind, that the definition of 'really bad' in country South Africa in the 70s was the local Priest's twin sons who rode motorbikes and smoked dope! A very low benchmark for rebellion.

After I took up smoking, the group of smokers sat in a grassy park, with a good vantage point to spot any nosy teachers or parents, where we'd sit in a circle and puff away. We smoked our cigarettes in the same place, at the same time every day. It was our own little ritual.

Now smoking was not particularly pleasant (especially in the beginning of habit formation) but the habit was reinforced by the slightly daring nature of the forbidden activity, the repetition in the same place at the same time, and because we had social support, by smoking with the same group of friends.

Of course, smoking is not just a psychologically addictive habit; it's extremely physically addictive. In fact, some researchers liken its addictive ability to heroin. So, once we left school, we didn't just give up smoking because it was not being reinforced by the context and the companionship of our friends. We continued to smoke because it was now an **ingrained habit**. Also, at that time, there was less social stigma about smoking, and most young people smoked. If you got in a plane, or went into a restaurant or pub, everyone smoked. It was normal.

So, a couple of years late when I was in my early 20s, I decided to give up smoking. I had given up smoking before in the past, but as soon as I socialised with my friends, I'd have one cigarette, then sooner or later, I'd end up smoking a pack a day again.

Now, back then, I had never heard of the technique, but I used similar principles to give up smoking. So, if I was going to give up smoking long term, I had to do two things; one was to **replace the habit** with something else, and the other was to **change the context and cues** that triggered the habit.

First, I changed the context and the cues. As discussed previously, it's often easier to break long standing habits in concert with a change in environment, such as a move, change in jobs or something similar. I had recently tired of partying in the city, and had moved back to my parents' farm. Thus, I had changed my environment. I no longer lived in a share house in the city with smokers. I lived in the country with my parents, neither of whom smoked. Although they did not try and stop me smoking (as I was now over 21, an adult and objected to any parental influence on what I did), they certainly made their disapproval obvious.

Another thing I did was to **change the cues**. I had never been one of those smokers who lit up first thing in the morning, but I liked a cigarette with my first coffee. I also used to like smoking when I went out, and particularly when having a beer. So I gave up alcohol and gave up going out. This was not as difficult as it may seem as I was living on a rural property 50km away from the city, where all my friends lived. If I wanted to go and party, I had to borrow a car from my parents, drive to the city, and then drive home. I hate driving, particularly at night. Giving up drinking was also relatively simple (at that time) as my parents don't drink either, so there was no alcohol in the house, and if I wanted any---I had to drive to the shop. Also, I was not working at the time, and didn't have enough money to go and spend it on booze.

BREAKING THE BOOZE HABIT

Finally, whenever I wanted a cigarette, **I replaced it with something else**. I decided to take up jogging. This was particularly effective in the mornings. Now I'm not a natural runner, and was one of those children who used to hide in the library to get out of any sort of sport (although, being of the older generation, participation in sport was compulsory). I'm not very good at sport either, I've zero coordination and I run very slowly.

I seriously sucked at running. I couldn't run more than about 500m without stopping in complete exhaustion, face bright red and sweat running down my face, puffing like an 80 year old with emphysema, and wanting to throw up. Some people begin running, and take to it like the proverbial duck. I took to it like the proverbial rock.

After a few weeks, I joined a running club. I loved going to the running club, and no-one smoked, so I was not exposed to any smoking behaviour. Unfortunately, they all loved beer, but that is another story---and another habit. By joining the running club, I got my social fix (much as I loved my parents, I needed the companionship of people my own age), my running was encouraged, and I hung around with people who were extremely anti-smoking.

The less I smoked, the healthier I felt. I remember the first time when I started to smell things again. I used to wear contact lenses, and I remember to this day, pouring the contact solution into the little case, and smelling the chemical smell of it. I had never known that it had a smell. Food also began to taste better. The more I ran, the less I wanted to smoke.

After a while, I discovered that the last thing I wanted after running was a cigarette. I had changed **replaced the habit** with something else (running) and changed the **context** and the **cues** that triggered the desire to smoke. I have maintained not smoking now for nearly 38 years.

Incentives and disincentives

Once you have identified your real habit, why you want to break it, and what rewards you get for your habit, you might also want to give yourself some incentives for giving up or disincentives for continuing. So, what do you really want? That's not that easy to find out.

For example, sometimes when I want to lose a couple of kilograms, I use clothes shopping as an incentive, telling myself that if I lose say 3kg, I can buy some new clothes. The problem is, I can go and buy clothes any time I feel like it, so it's not much of an incentive.

And if you set up disincentives, especially if they kick in every time you lapse (and you will lapse), then you are likely to give up the whole idea the first time you have to 'pay'.

So, for an incentive, you need to find out something **you really want**, and something that you will have to **work towards**. For example, if you want a new computer or IPhone, but have got plenty of money (or are not too fussy about credit card debt), and are inclined to impulse shop, it's not much point making this your incentive. The next time you browse Amazon, you will probably pull out the old plastic and buy the thing anyway. However, if you do not have much money, and don't believe in buying things on credit, putting some money into a jar or savings account every time you are good, could be a great incentive. This type of incentive works even better if someone else administers it, or if you use the **reverse incentive** method (put a largish sum of money away, and each time you lapse, you have to take some out, or give it to a charity you don't like, etc.). This also works better if another person manages it, unless you are exceptionally honest with yourself (most of us lie to ourselves more than anyone else.)

Also, incentives can start off small, and add up, and they don't have to be physical. They can also be psychological and stepwise incentives, along the same principles as goal-setting.

What do I mean by that?

Well, you can progress towards your goal by moving forward in bite-sized pieces. It's like planning to write a book or thesis. Writing 100,000 or more words is a horribly daunting task (well, it is to me, I get bored quickly), but if you break it down, into say, 1000 words a day, or even a week, it becomes much more manageable. Unless you are me, in which case, maybe 100 words a day is more like it.

Also, using psychological methods, and **visibly marking your progress** towards your goal, you can also give yourself smaller rewards along the way; say a Swiss ice-cream at the end of a week that you didn't drink, or that you stuck to pre-arranged limit for drinking (say no more than 5 days a week, and no more than 4 alcohol units per day).

In this way, you can use a lot of the psychological lessons I have discussed in the previous chapters, to help you break your bad habits or make a good habit. Ok, let's get to the technique.

CHAPTER 7 THE TECHNIQUE

"Don't break the chain" **Jerry Seinfeld**

BREAKING THE HABIT OF HABITUAL DRINKING

How do you break a bad habit such as habitual drinking? Like me, I'm sure you have tried many times, and failed. Well, there IS a solution! But you have to work at it. This book is based on scientific research. It's not clickbait or a magic pill that will miraculously curb your cravings. Life doesn't work like that.

NOTE: please consult a medical professional first if you are seriously addicted to alcohol or other drugs.

Groups such as Alcoholics Anonymous offer an excellent environment and motivation.

These strategies can all form part of your own 'toolbox' to help you curb your drinking

BREAKING THE BOOZE HABIT

BASIC TASKS

1. **Identify the habit**
    a. **Change just ONE habit at a time** (don't just decide that you want to run a marathon, write a bestselling book, lose 20kg AND give up drinking all at once)
    b. If it is a big habit, **chunk it into smaller bits** and set yourself a **realistic deadline** which may be a year or longer, then daily and weekly goals (if you have been drinking every day for 20 years, and you don't want to give up entirely, you can always start with one less drink a week, or change the type of alcohol you drink)
    c. Know your emotional and physical **trigger points**
    d. Be prepared to take two steps forward and one back

2. **Identify Your Own Incentives**
    a. If you have been journaling (or even just thought really deeply) you know what floats your boat. A suggestion is to use small incentives for sticking to your goals for a week, larger rewards for a month, a really nice reward for a specific time (say 3 months) and something totally awesome for achieving the goal (sadly, Chris Hemsworth <insert fantasy person of your own choice> is unavailable and or not remotely interested in obscure middle-aged Australian academics)
    b. Rewards don't have to be concrete, they can be experiences, psychological, or anything else pleasurable
    c. I don't use disincentives (because I am inclined to cheat), but if you do, try and use something like the money jar. For example, if you want to give up smoking, put in a sum of money (the amount depends on how rich you are, but it is important to make it a sum that would hurt if you had to lose it), and you have to donate or lose a specified amount each time you lapse.
    d. It's also great to get other people (children, partners, friends or colleagues) to participate in your challenge. Group support is a proven technique to help people quit bad habits. As mentioned above, the AA is a great place to find like-minded people if you want to give up alcohol entirely.

BREAKING THE BOOZE HABIT

Find a Hobby: Hobbies are great for general mental health and are **enjoyable** (as long as it is a hobby that you actually like, if you are a hyperactive outdoor person such as me, it is not much point taking up needlework or scrapbooking, and vice versa for an indoor person, taking up rock climbing).

A new hobby that seems to be really popular is coloring-in books for adults. Some have really great patterns, and are a good way to keep your mind busy, in a meditative sort of way. Otherwise, you could do painting, writing, reading, gardening, whatever---

For me, I would really like to be more productive at night, the problem is, I am better at EVERYTHING in the morning; exercise, working, writing, running, working in the garden, etc---and all I really like doing at night is vegging. Perhaps I should move to somewhere that has really long daylight hours.

I can keep busy at all time when it is light---but as soon as it is dark, then I tend to find a spot on the couch, pour myself a glass of wine, and watch Food Network (which makes me hungry, so I snack) and/or read mindless crime novels.

THE STUFF.

Ok, to put the technique into practice you need the following:

- *A wall calendar*
- *Some star stickers*
- *Any other types of stickers – go wild*
- *Different colour pens/ kokis*
- *A system of incentives and disincentives*

The Calendar

You need a calendar; one of those wall calendars with has a page for each month, with a square for each day. A pretty or motivational calendar is great, but you can also use a year planner, print your own or buy ours.

Some people are motivated by beautiful scenery (mine has pictures of beautiful National Parks), or by inspirational quotes, or by people who you want to look like (if your goal is fitness or weight loss) or even by people you would like to impress (hmm, shirtless firemen or football players).

101

BREAKING THE BOOZE HABIT

You also need to put the calendar where you can see it every day. For me, it's in my bedroom, but you might want to hang it up in a more public place, like the kitchen.

Publicly documenting your successes is also an excellent way of maintaining motivation. If you are really masochistic, you can share daily updates on Facebook (probably lose all your friends from sheer boredom).

On the top of the calendar, write down **your goals for that month**.

For example, mine used to say:

- No more than 14 alcohol units per week
- No more than 4 alcohol units one any one day
- At least two alcohol free days per week

As I have given up drinking entirely, I don't have a heading, but I write my weight down every week, and if I have meditated or written something.

Stickers

You need to buy some stickers.

My stickers		
No alcohol on a day	green star	★
Less than 2 AU* on a day	orange star	★
2 - 4 AU in one day	a poor blank square	☐
Over 4 AU in a day	a black mark	☒
Minor weekly goal (<14AU)	smiley sticker	☺
No alcohol for a week	Special shiny smiley star	
*=AU Alcohol Units		

Nowadays, there's an awesome choice in stickers. I used to use stars, but got creative (because I couldn't buy ordinary stars anymore) so now I use smiley faces, butterflies and big shiny glitter stars. You can also buy "bad" stickers, like skulls or other stuff (these are harder to get hold of, newsagents seem to prefer to stock cutesy stickers). Perhaps put a cutesy sticker upside down. When I'm 'bad', I draw black crosses, or write in big letters, 'BAD'.

BREAKING THE BOOZE HABIT

The main point is to identify what each sticker stands for. These stickers are your visual mini goals.

Note: no cheating, and use proper AU. You might need to measure drinks or 'get' one of those pub glasses, with the 100ml line--- you can paint a line using a glass marker pen.)

I also wrote down each day that I drank exactly how much and of what I drank. For example, 1B/2W (3AU) means that I had 1 bottle of mid-strength beer and 2 glasses of wine (I count an alcohol unit of 100ml as one glass); therefore, I'd drunk 3 alcohol units that day. At the end of the week, I tallied up the total for each day and wrote it in a different colour pen. If I didn't drink at all, I got a special sticker.

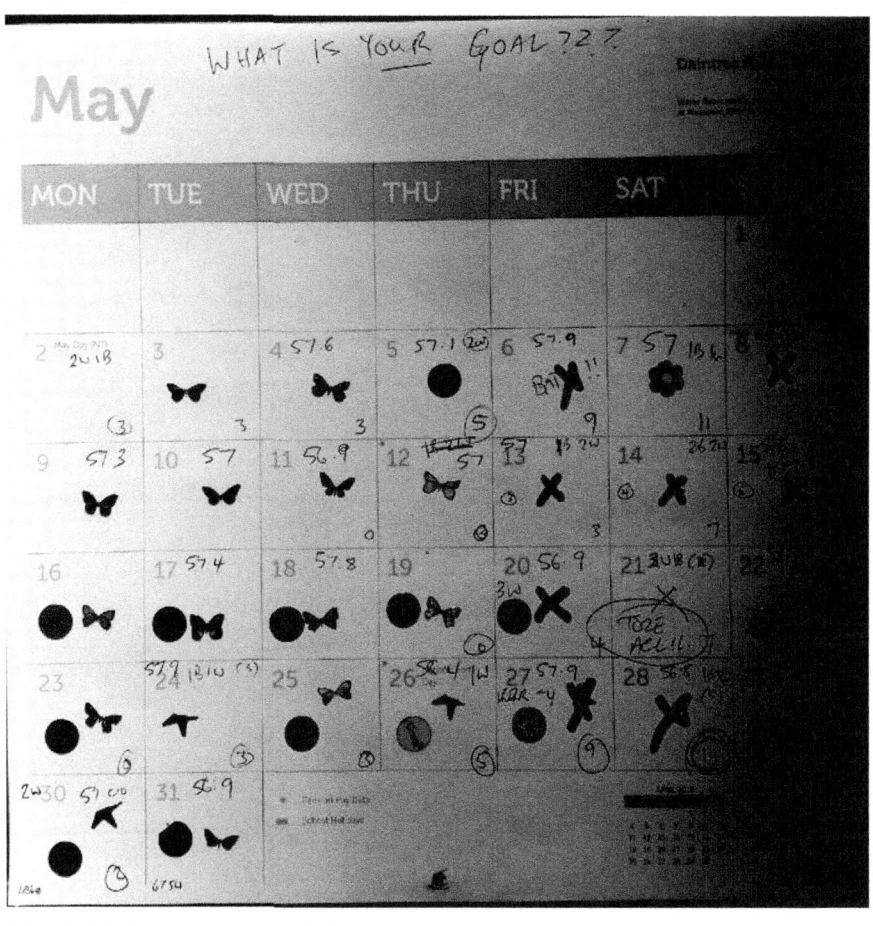

May 2016: beginning no drinking

BREAKING THE BOOZE HABIT

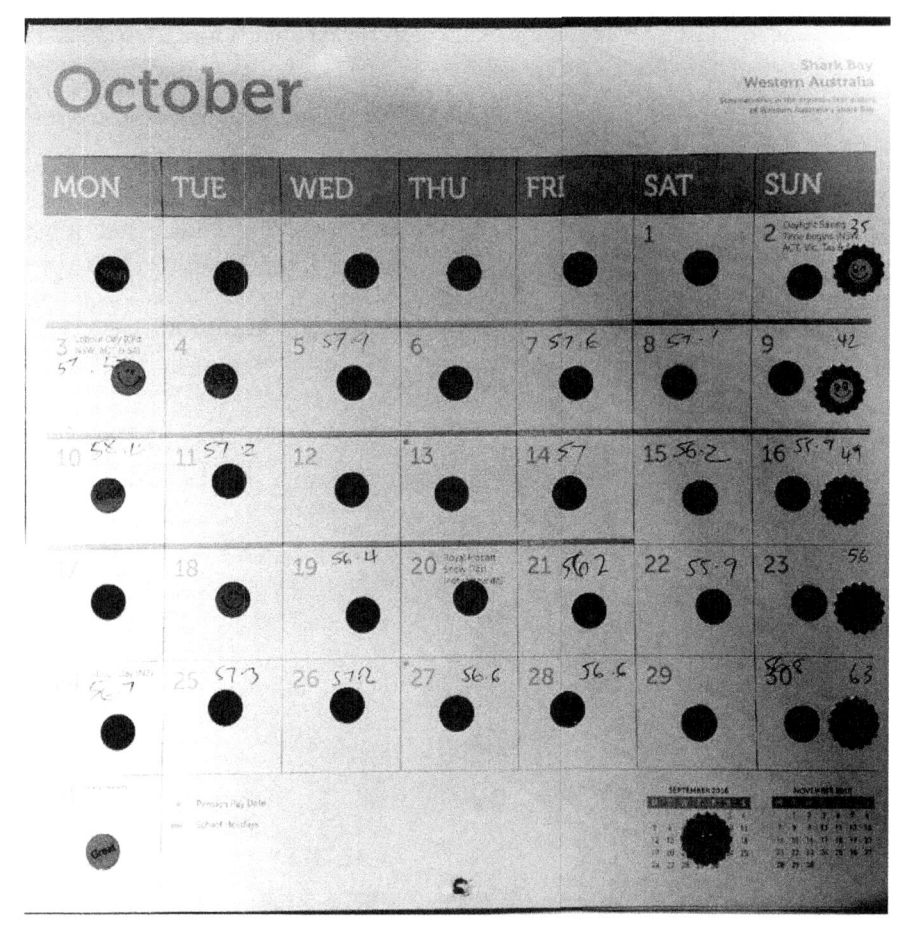

October 2016: Unbroken chain

Examples of giving up other types of bad habits

I'll give some examples of some common bad habits, and how you can use the same technique to address these.

Smoking

Giving up smoking is not easy. But this technique can help you get there. First of all, giving up smoking should be the end goal, and the aim of the technique is to slowly minimise your smoking until you achieve your goal. Also, I suggest that you use quit smoking help at the same time (like nicotine patches etc.). You also need to make the choice, are you going to quit smoking slowly, or cold turkey? There are advantages and disadvantages to both of these.

104

BREAKING THE BOOZE HABIT

Note: please seek medical advice before using any medications, and preferably before trying to give up smoking.

Jarryd is a colleague of mine. In his mid-30s, he desperately wanted to quit smoking, but had failed so many times. He mostly tried to quit cold turkey, but this time, he has decided to do it in a slower manner

To use the technique, Jarryd took a week to write down how many cigarettes he smoked every day, what time and how he was feeling. He told me that this was a pain, but he did it (though whinged a lot).

Sure, he probably forgot some, but at least he had some idea of his trigger points and weak areas.

You can try keeping a smoking diary for a week, or if you could also use the calendar, and just write how many cigarettes you had each day.

Jarryd figured that he smoked about 24 cigarettes a day (or 168 per week). His goal was to give up smoking completely in 3 months. This worked out to about 12 weeks, and meant that he had to smoke 2 cigarettes less per day (14 less per week) for the first week, meaning that he smoked 22 cigarettes a day for the first week.

The second week, he chose to smoke 20 cigarettes instead of 22, and so on and so on. He figured that cutting down by two cigarettes a day (and doing this over a week) would make the quitting relatively easy to achieve.

However, if you think this is too much too soon, then cut down 1 a week (or the equivalent) over 6 months or even longer. You've probably been smoking for a long time anyway.

This is a good technique when looking at a long term habit, such as smoking or weight gain. It took a long time to get the problem, so it isn't going to go away in a week.

Jarryd set up a sticker system and gave himself a yellow smiley face for smoking 22 cigarettes or less, an orange star for smoking 22 – 24, and a black mark for going over 24. He also wrote down the actual number he had smoked per day and added it up.

At the end of the week, if he had stuck to his goal of 14 less, then he got a special star and if he smoked even fewer, then he got an even more special sticker (he used car stickers---much more manly than shiny stars, lol).

The important number is the one at the end of the week. You might have days when you smoke more than 24 cigarettes, but it's the total that matters; if you lapse, then try and cut down the next day.

Jarryd also practiced distracting himself. Cravings only last about 7 minutes, so he went for a walk, had a cup of coffee, or just stayed in the office. Smoking is banned all over campus, so it was a hassle to walk half a kilometer to an area where smoking is permitted. He also went for drives with his wife, which made not smoking easier, because she hated smoking and it was banned in the car.

If you hang around people who don't smoke (or drink), you will feel less like smoking (or drinking).

Weight Loss

You can use this technique to address the bad habits that lead to weight gain, for example, snacking, eating junk food or drinking soda.

Now, your end goal is to lose weight, say 10kg, but you need to identify the reasons why you put on weight in the first place. For some people, this is easy, just give up sodas like Coke or Pepsi---but **do not substitute with diet soft drinks**---they are worse for you, totally stuff up your insulin levels and make you hungry.

Tasmin wanted to lose weight, not that much, just about 10kg. She had put on weight after having her 2nd baby and it had hung around, for the next decade, sitting there around her hips and middle, stubbornly refusing to go.

Tasmin did a bit of soul searching as to why she was a bit overweight. Now, many people are happy with how their bodies are, no matter how big they are, but Tasmin's self-confidence was tied to her weight. She probably could do with a bit of counselling about self-esteem issues, but she really wanted to shift that 10kg. She had also split up with her partner a couple of years ago, and felt ready to re-enter the dating scene.

She identified that one of the major reasons she put on weight, was that after dinner and then putting the kids to bed, she would carry on eating, almost mindlessly. This snacking was also related to another bad habit, drinking too much wine (her and me both).

First Tasmin kept a food diary for a week, using an online app, MyFitnessPal. Like the others, she tried to be honest and weight her food. She was quite horrified at how many extra calories she was eating at night. Also, another issue was that she was not eating properly during the day, so when dinner came, she ate it too fast, then was still hungry.

Tasmin had a lot of work to do about her relationship with food, and also scheduling healthy meals during the day. But, first things first. She decided to deal with her after dinner snacking.

Now, she wasn't going to give up snacking at first, but she was going to give up snacking on unhealthy things, particularly Doritos corn chips, which were her favourite food.

So, she set up a star system, if she ate no snacks at all after dinner, then she got a gold star; if she ate healthy snacks only (not too many) then she got a green star, and if she only ate one unhealthy snack (a small amount), then she got an brown star. At the end of a good week (gold and green stars), she gave herself a special star and allowed herself a treat (not a snack, something like a visit to the hairdresser or a new book).

Be careful if you use this system not to cheat---I once tried this and easily gave up snacking---because I just ate more dinner AND added dessert, which I don't normally eat. Did I lose weight? Nope.

Tasmin also made sure to keep busy, and not to let herself get too bored.

At the beginning of the exercise, Tasmin wrote her weight down on the calendar. She also weighed herself (at the same time of day) every Monday and Friday. Most people who maintain a healthy weight weigh themselves regularly. Also, if you like, write down your measurements.

What is important here is the trend, not the daily fluctuations. It is common that your weight may differ by up to 2kg in a week, depending on what you have eaten the day before, how much liquid you have drunk and your hormonal levels. This is also a good technique to analyse your own weight fluctuations (which might be much more or less, as we are all different).

There are thousands of other weight loss techniques, but an important thing to remember is:

You took a long time to put on the weight, if you lose it too quickly, you are almost guaranteed to put it back on.

Combining any weight loss diet with exercise is also essential. I know some people cannot do strenuous exercise, for health or other reasons, but any exercise is better than none. They even do weight training in aged care homes, with people who are aged in their 80s and older. Exercise has huge benefits for everyone---if you can, get a dog, then you will be forced to exercise (and it will benefit the dog too).

Watching too much TV or too much time on Social Media

Come on, how much TV do you actually watch? Most people lie about this, saying, oh I only watch a couple of hours a week. Yeah right. Most people watch a couple of hours a night.

And if we are not watching TV, how much time are we spending on our computers, smart phones, playing games or tablets? There are apps that will tell us to the second how much time we are wasting---and that is true, it is wasted time.

If you do decided to cut down on your media use, try and work out in the weeks before beginning the habit breaking, to identify how many hours you spend watching various media, what times, and where. It may very well be in the evenings between 6pm and 8pm or it may be other times, depending on your own schedule.

So, say you spend 4 hours a day on various media, and you want to cut down to 2 hours a day or less. Then, give yourself a special star for no media, a different star for 1 hour and a 'bad' sticker for 2 hours or more. At the end of the week, you can tally up your media watching and give yourself a special star---or decide to do better the following week.

You can also give yourself different coloured or types of stars for the type of media. I'm certain there would be Facebook 'like' stickers or other social media logos available!

Being too critical (or other emotional bad habits)

Ok, all these habits are concrete things that we do every time, over and over, but what about emotional bad habits?

Straun has been happily married for nearly 15 years---well, as happy as a couple can be anyway. His wife Melinda frequently comments that when he watches TV, he criticises everything. Whether it is the news, or a gardening or cooking program, or a documentary, there is inevitably something about it that irritates him. And his constant criticism irritates Melinda, so much so that when the TV goes on, she goes out of the room. This is causing problems in their relationship.

Straun however has taken Melinda's comments to heart, and has acknowledged that he has a very bad habit of being constantly critical (and not just of TV). But he also realises that this is not always a conscious thing he does---in other words, it is a HABIT.

So how can Straun use the technique to stop his constant criticism?

Well, he can first of all try and be more mindful of what he is doing, especially when engaging in a rather mindless pursuit, such as watching TV. He can also get Melinda's help, and ask her to (nicely) tell him when he is being too critical (I don't really recommend this, as in my experience, it leads to arguments and defensiveness).

He can also try and watch TV that he enjoys. If the news annoys him so much, then he can watch something else.

He might use the technique to give himself a star if he is not critical at all, a different star if he only criticises a few times, and a black mark if he does it like usual.

Because this habit is something that affects others in the household, he is going to have to be a bit patient---as is Melinda. She is going to have to support him, and even if he has been very 'good' in a week, to reward him somehow. I'm sure they can figure out some mutually acceptable rewards.

Examples of some Good Habits (and mini goals)

Regular exercise

Most of us would probably like to do more exercise, even if it is just incidental exercise, like walking more often. One of the (few) things that I have managed to stick at for a long time is running.

Now you may ask, am I naturally good at sport? Do I enjoy exercise? No, not for a millisecond. When I was a child (which, according to my sons, is about a thousand years ago); at the beginning of each new term at school, we were forced to participate in a unique form of torture, also known as being chosen for sporting teams. Compulsory team sport, which, by the way, I loathe and at which I am particularly inept.

So, as us the poor little victims (aka, potential team members) stood in line, two miniature Stalins or Pol Pots (every school has some, they are brilliant at sport and always the team captains) would cast their beady little eyes on the pathetic row of girls either hoping to be chosen or hoping *not* to be chosen.

Now, unfortunately, and totally belying my lack of sporting ability, I *look* very athletic, so when I went to a new school (which happened quite often), I was often chosen **first** to join a team; especially in some odious sport like hockey, which I'm certain is only played by sadists who enjoy whacking weak and vulnerable creatures, like me, on the shins.

In a very short time (usually about 5 minutes) the rest of the team and of course, the despot captain, soon realised that athletic **appearance** does not correlate with athletic **ability**, and I displayed an exceptionally slow running speed, an inclination to lurk in the far reaches of the field and hope no-one noticed, a rather anarchic attitude to the rules and a complete and utter lack of any coordination or ability to play any ball sports (yes, even those). I've no idea what 'offside' actually means, but that term got yelled at me an awful lot.

So, come the following term, I'd be there, with all the other rejects, while the team captains argued amongst themselves about who was the least objectionable; while we shuffled our feet forlornly, on one hand hoping not be chosen last (social death) or on the other, hoping that they'd reject us all outright, so we could go back to our true home (the library).

As mentioned, I have absolutely no coordination. I like to go to music festivals, and at some, you can participate in all sorts of fun stuff, like dancing and singing classes, which despite my total lack of talent, are great fun. Once I was standing at the back of a huge marquee with my youngest son Robin. I don't recall his age, but he must have been pre-teen or he would not have been seen dead accompanying his mother to a dance class.

Anyway, I was having a wonderful time, dancing to some two-step or Ghanaian dubstep rap or something, when he turned to me and said, *'Mom, your dancing sucks.'*

I turned to him and said, 'yes, I know, but look, there are plenty of bad dancers.'

With that he replied, *'Yes, but you're the WORST.'*

So, given my complete lack of sporting ability, why did I decide to take up running, and have managed to keep at it for 30 years? And how did the lessons that I learned from this translate to me developing the technique?

Obviously, I persevered at running because of the multiple incentives. But incentives don't always work that well. So what about disincentives? Well anyone who has run for any length of time will tell you that you can become 'hooked' and have to keep at it. Is this true? Can you become 'addicted' to exercise'? Now I'm not too keen on much of this modern talk of 'sex addiction' or 'internet addiction' or whatever. It all seems a bit of a copout to me. Although exercise is not 'addictive' in the true sense, it certainly can lead to improved mood, and other benefits, which may to some extent be considered a sort of dependence.

For example, exercise can trigger the brain to produce its own drugs; endorphins, encephalins and endocannabinoids (yes, *those* cannabinoids). It's hypothesized that endocannabinoids lead to what is termed 'the runner's high', which is a feeling of wellbeing after exercise.

But most importantly, regular exercise is a HABIT. And the brain likes its habits. If, like most people, you clean your teeth upon waking, and miss this one day, you certainly miss it and crave it. The brain likes its routines. Thinking is hard work and uses up valuable calories (not, you won't lose any weight by thinking) so it makes short cuts, or habits, to save having to think. Imagine if you had to think about every time you cleaned your teeth, or rode a bicycle.

Exercise also has a biological basis. Humans are the only predominately bipedal mammal (walks on two legs). When long droughts began to hit our ancestral forests, we moved into the African Savannah. Now, humans are pretty puny creatures, compared to the large, carnivorous mammals of the Pleistocene[94]. These things were huge, and had enormous teeth---and we were definitely part of *their* 'Paleo' diets. Running was a life saver for early humans, who unlike all other mammals, can regulate their internal temperature by sweating, and have greater endurance. We also ran to catch our own prey (well, we probably made traps and hid behind trees, as most animals are much faster than we are, but I'm sure that *sometimes* if we saw a very slow, old, sick animal, we might be able run and catch it, that is, if a large carnivorous mammal didn't get to it before we did).

So a disincentive to stopping exercise is dependence.

The results of many academic studies indicate that aerobic exercise has anti-depressant and anti-anxiety effects---and it helps make the body more resilient against stress. Recent research also indicates that not only does exercise have a beneficial effect on the cardiovascular system (thus protecting against heart-attacks and strokes) but also helps keep the brain healthy---it could even prevent Alzheimer's.

Running helps me tremendously with mood regulation. I am an anxious person at times (others might say, all the time), and worry unnecessarily. I'm prone to catastrophizing, especially about health. Most people get a twinge of pain, or see a spot, and think, I've pulled a muscle, or I've got indigestion from too many chilies; but not me. I immediately diagnose myself with something fatal and painful, and start planning my eulogy, what songs will play at my funeral, and how long before I must book the hospice.

Running helps me curb that over-thinking; and also I have what my oldest son (who inherited this) calls 'the attention span of a gnat'; and I found running made me not only healthier, less anxious---but better able to concentrate.

I also stuck to running because I liked the competitive aspect and how I kept improving. Participating in fun runs was even better. In fun runs, you don't have to be good to win prizes, you just have to be lucky and get your name pulled out of a hat. Even better, sports like Parkrun or cross country will give you prizes based on how often you turn up, or if you beat your own times!

Long before I thought of the technique, I used to write down how far I had run, per day, and per week. Back then, this was pre-internet, so I wrote on the calendar in the kitchen (which annoyed my mother as that was where she wrote family birthdays). Nowadays of course, you can chart your running using any number of apps, which will give you kilometers run, pace per kilometer and calories burned (usually rather a dodgy figure).

Likewise, another colleague, Kylie, has a desk job, where she often sits for long periods, sometimes over two hours without getting up.

There are lots and lots of apps that Kylie can use to set a daily step goal, and these also give all sorts of interesting information. But if Kylie is like most of us, she has dozens of apps on her phone, and can't even remember downloading them. I have mine organised into pages, type and colour, but I am weird (at least according to my family and friends).

So Kylie can get a pedometer, or put a good app on the main page of her phone. Some, like MapMyWalk, Strava and Runkeeper are awesome and incredibly accurate, but they do use GPS, and everyone knows that smartphone batteries are like mayflies---they have a lifespan measured in minutes, and nothing chews up a battery like GPS.

I have a Samsung Galaxy S5 (I know it's an old phone, at least in phone years, but it works well), and it has an inbuilt app which measures steps (very accurately too, I've tested it on known distances). It's not that accurate walking over mountains, but that will probably not be in most people's daily routines.

Kylie set herself a step goal of 15,000 steps per day, and used an app and a pedometer (which she got for free in some government initiative aimed at improving health). She also wrote down her weight at least twice a week; even though her goal was not weight loss, she wanted to see if upping her exercise did anything for her weight, which she felt was a tad high.

She gave herself a gold star for over 15k, a green star for 10 – 15k, and no stars for under 10k. Like the other people, her real goal was the weekly goal, of 105k, so even if she had some days when she didn't attain her step goal, she could just walk more the next day.

Walking more can be very easy. You can set a timer to get up; you can take the stairs instead of the lift; you can park further away from work (or even walk if you live close enough) and you could join a walking group or Parkrun.

After Kylie's three months, she was so pumped; she had lost 2kg without even trying, and was even secretly planning to start running. She also bought herself some great looking workout clothes.

Creative habits

For creating habits, for example, I try and write something every day; I write down how many words I've written each day (in a different colour pen to the alcohol tally). I don't give myself a star for every day that I write, but I could do if I wanted.

Then, at the end of the week, I tally up the amount of words I've written, and if it's >5000 words, then I give myself a different, pretty star. For each 10,000 words, I give myself a special shiny sticker.

Hints and tips

Do the sticking and writing in the morning of the next day, because if you are trying not to drink at night, and give yourself a star, you might still lapse.

All this stuff sounds like it is a lot of work, but it isn't. It literally takes about 5 minutes (if that), but is closer to 1 minute. It takes hardly any time in the mornings to put a sticker on a calendar or write down how much you drank the night before.

If doing something like writing down the amount of words written, this just means that I go into the document that I'm writing, and look at the word count at the bottom of the page.

It's so simple and quick, it's child's play.

Incentives

Do you remember when you were in school, and your teacher gave you a gold star for achievement? It was a wonderful feeling. You felt special.

This still works. Even if you give yourself the reward.

When you give yourself a minor star, or a special star, it feels good. It feels like you have achieved something.

This is based on the psychology of incentive.

If you do this for long enough, filling in the calendar, and sticking the stars becomes a habit in itself---but a good self-monitoring habit.

And it's exactly like Seinfeld's chain---the more stars you have and the longer you stick to your regime, the more incentive you have to maintain it and not break the chain.

Then, when you achieve a bigger goal, one of your minor goals, say to write 10,000 words, then you can give yourself a treat, say allowing yourself to buy something small. This feels good. It feels like you've **earned** the reward. Even just the big end of week star is a reward in itself.

Why is this? Well, if you just go out every day and buy yourself things, then they don't feel that good. They are just things. But if you have waited for something, and worked towards achieving it and waited some time, then it's much more pleasant.

And of course, you don't have to reward yourself with **things.** You can reward yourself with a massage, or a yoga class, or a trip somewhere. I'm doing a lot of renovating around my garden at the moment, and although I enjoy it, I give myself a small reward, say I can relax on my lounger with a book and a non-alcoholic beer when I finish, or I walk up to the local pub and listen to some music. These are simple pleasures, but are lovely.

Of course, we are all different. Your pleasures might be something totally different than mine; they could be going to the movies, visiting a friend, or just having a nap without feeling guilty.

The point is, you are allowing yourself a **small pleasure, without feeling guilty**; allowing yourself a small pleasure that you have earned.

When you have achieved a really big goal (say, publishing a book, or losing a lot of weight) then you can reward yourself with something big. It does not have to be financial; but make it worthwhile.

Nowadays, children are too often praised for the slightest thing, but when I was a child, you only got praise for really hard work, or a significant achievement. We competed with one another for these small rewards. I still have certificates from primary school (over 40 years ago) praising me for getting 100% on a spelling test, or coming 3rd in the high jump at the athletics carnival.

HOW DOES IT WORK (BACK TO THE SCIENCE)

Neuroscience

We read that our brain is lazy and likes to keep all its energy for things like maintaining our breathing and heartbeat. Thus it creates habits as shortcuts for having to think about non-essential, often repeated actions---'neurons that wire together, fire together', creating a metaphorical rut in your brain---or a habit.

You've identified that your drinking is habitual, linked to specific times and places. Often, you are unaware of how much you are drinking, and are not mindful when drinking. Your brain has programmed a rut; its 6pm, wine time.

Now, with the journal and the calendar, you are forcing your brain to actively think about your drinking (rather than the 2am obsessive thoughts, 'why am I such an idiot, tomorrow I am *definitely* going to give up drinking'). By **breaking the procedural memory** of doing the same thing in the same way every day, you have forced the action of drinking into conscious awareness (or explicit or declarative memory). You have also forced it out of its default selective attention mode. If any of you have tried active listening, you will know how very difficult and exhausting it is.

The brain will resist this; as I said, it is lazy and likes its habits. You need to take it in hand and show it who is boss! Actually, it IS the boss, but you (some parts of the brain) have some power over (other) parts of it.

The anterior cingulate cortex and orbitofrontal cortex are both involved in habit formation, but they are also involved in reward seeking and incentives. If your reward is not tangible, but is the feeling of **satisfaction** at seeing a row or even a whole week or month of stars, this can often be of **stronger motivation** than a purely financial reward.

Then, the dorsolateral prefrontal cortex is related to **planning, action, decision making and memory.** You choosing to deal with your habitual drinking, then buying this book and planning how you will go about solving the problem, are all things that the dorsolateral prefrontal cortex specialises in.

The amygdala is related to **cue anticipation and emotional memory**; forming associations between the pleasant nature of an experience (a good Shiraz on a cold night) and the cues that give rise to that experience (pouring your first wine after dinner).

Psychology

Learning the habit of drinking is both associative (associated with specific actions, times and cues) and script based (our internal script tells us when to perform a certain behaviour). To emphasize what was discussed in Chapter 3, "a habit is comprised of three major elements: **repetition, automaticity** and **stable (or consistent) contexts; it is prompted by situational cues, repeated in a stable context**".

We are beginning to break the habit of drinking, which we have learned by repeating the behaviour in consistent situations so that it has become automatic. By thinking about the behaviour, using mindfulness and journaling, we have broken the cycle of automaticity.

By using the calendar and the stars method, we are first of all, **creating a NEW habit** of daily updating our alcohol consumption (if any); and secondly, we are **breaking the automaticity of drinking**. Automaticity is characterised by the lack of awareness, control, and conscious intent. By **forcing ourselves to think** about how much we have consumed, measuring this, and totaling it at the end of every day, we are breaking the automaticity of drinking.

We also saw that information campaigns and top down (prescriptive) methods of changing behaviour often do not succeed, and may backfire. Voluntary behaviour change on the other hand, is much more effective, but it has to be maintained or the brain will slip back into its bad habits.

I like to **read about the negative impacts of alcohol** on my body and mind, which helps to reinforce me not drinking. You can also remember (even using deliberate false memories) about times that you drank too much, and felt terrible. For example, I could bring back memories of the panic attack I had one night after drinking too much, and thought I was dying of a heart attack. Even though I knew it was a panic attack, this helped reinforce that alcohol can have serious impacts on the heart.

By reading (or watching, whatever type of media you are most comfortable with) stories and information on the negative impacts of alcohol, you are **priming your brain** to see alcohol in a negative light.

I deliberately avoid articles that promote alcohol, even though this could be considered 'cherry picking' information to suit my own biases. I know that the best salesperson to motivate me is ME. If someone else tells me that I *should* (or *should not)* be doing something, then this triggers my inner rebel, and I often do the opposite (as can often result from fear-based campaigns).

Other ways of changing your habitual behaviour is to think of the **comfort, cleanliness and cost**. Drinking is pleasant (hence comfortable) but if you drink too much it is both uncomfortable and unclean (if I drink too much, it gives me both diarrhea and vomiting). Looking at comfort in another way, if I don't buy any alcohol and have none in the house, then it is beneficial for the cost (alcohol is very expensive) and it is a hassle to go to the bottle shop and buy more (thus it is uncomfortable).

Incentive and disincentive

Obviously, you need to establish your goal before you can use the calendar method. This might be to drink below a certain amount, on certain days only, or not drink at all. Of course, your goals have to be **measurable**. You can't just say that your goal is 'to be happier' or 'to drink less'. Instead, you could have a goal to smile at 10 strangers a day, and not to be rude to shop assistants, or to write in a gratefulness diary every day. Perhaps if you are a heavy drinker, you could have an initial goal of drinking only light beer, or drinking less than 20AU per week for a month, and then slowly reducing your consumption.

Honesty is also essential (especially if you live alone, if you live with others, they will probably see you breaking your goals---like having a drink on a Monday night when you are not supposed to) and take you to task for giving yourself a star on the calendar. Anyway, the worst type of lying is to yourself.

Now that you have your goal, you can use **incentive and disincentives** to ensure that you **stick to your goal**. These work really well with the calendar and stars method. There is an intrinsic incentive to be gained by looking at a run of stars, or from sticking to your goal for the week, especially if this is maintained over some time. We also saw that intrinsic incentive works much better than financial incentives, in breaking habits, and maintaining progress towards your goals. I find that if I have, say, 3 weeks of unbroken no drinking (**don't break the chain**), easily **visualised** on my calendar, then I am far less motivated to have a drink, and mess up my pretty run/chain/galaxy of stars.

One way that I also keep motivation is to write in a prominent place (on the calendar, and/or as I do, on my bathroom mirror) a list of reasons why alcohol is 'bad' for me. Obviously your list will be unique to yourself, but mine are, '**health, wealth, weight, sleep, psychology, spirituality, gut** and **relationships**'.

Alcohol is bad for my health, costs me a lot of money, makes me put on weight, impacts on my sleep (and I love sleeping), interferes with my meditation regime, is bad for my mental health, as I feel far less anxious when I don't drink (even though it is a temporary fix, I feel worse in the long run), gives me diarrhea and is negative for my relationships because when I drink I tend to argue with people.

Self-monitoring

One of the major ways that the calendar and stars methods works is that it triggers **vigilant control (monitoring)**. This heightens **conscious awareness**, which breaks the cycle of automaticity and environmental cues. Vigilant control and paying attention to your drinking by sticking a star on the calendar, and counting your drinks, forces you to think about what you are doing. Together with mindful drinking, vigilant control keeps your drinking from becoming habitual.

Any time you begin a new behaviour (or replace an old behaviour with something else), you draw attention to the behaviour. Putting stickers on the calendar **highlights** the behaviour, and makes it easier to immediately and **visually recognise** whether you have stuck to your behavioural goals. Because you have put the calendar in a place where you cannot help but see it every day, it's always **in your face**. If it's public, all the better. You will find soon enough that your partner, flatmates or children will take you to task for not sticking to your goals---just the same as I used to do with my sons, especially when one of them was not pulling his weight with his household chores.

Also, when you monitor the **outcomes** of your behaviour (say, weight loss, or reduction in blood sugar levels, or diarising that you feel healthier because you have cut down on drinking), you can **observe** your progress towards your goal. The calendar is an immediately visible way of **tracking your progress over time**. I even keep calendars from the previous year, where I can track certain things (such as what I weigh) over longer periods.

I find this really useful for things like alcohol consumption, as I can monitor over a long time what I drink, and see if I'm drinking too much, and need to cut down. It doesn't work the other way round; I think it's cheating to say, oh, I think I'm drinking too little, time to have a few more drinks.

You can also use it to further **analyse** the habit that you wish to break, and perhaps to **modify** your goal. For example, before I gave up drinking entirely, I gave myself stickers for cutting down on drinking. Looking back over the month, I saw a clear **pattern** emerging. I tended to have stars on Monday, Tuesday and Wednesday (sometimes Thursday) but frequently have no stars or comments such as "BAD" on weekends.

Obviously I needed to do something about drinking on weekends. Why do I tend to drink more on weekends? What circumstances are different on weekends to weekdays? What did I need to **change** over weekends?

I also use this technique to give myself other goals, and to monitor my performance of these. Say you have a goal to write a 100,000 book, if you write on the calendar every time you stick to your minor goals (i.e. 1000 words a day) then you can **observe** the word count adding up. For example, one month I took part in a challenge to do a minimum of 10,000 steps per day. The calendar made tracking this really easy. When giving up drinking (even now) I frequently think about lapsing. But, as I see the stars and days add up and make a longer chain, I think, what a waste; or how could I break that pretty pattern?

Finally, if you monitor the **context** in which the behaviour occurs, then you can see that you are sticking to your new habit in the same way (encouraging stability of context) which leads to habit formation. With my calendar, the longer I carry on, and the more stars I get, the less I want to give in and have a drink; even at times , such as when I was going through relationship problems, and I could easily have turned to alcohol to help me deal with the pain.

This technique works because it's **visual.** People are often more likely to notice visual cues than other cues.

Accrued success

Because it highlights **success**. And even more important, it highlights what is known as **accrued success. DON'T BREAK THE CHAIN!**

What is accrued success and how does this technique show it? Well, accrued success is not just *one* day without alcohol, or without smoking, or writing 500 words---it is two days, a week, two weeks, a month---**it's a run or a chain of little successes that add up to a BIG success.** The calendar, with its stars visually describes a run of success. Even more importantly, when you have weeks without many stars, it shows other weeks where you *stuck* to your goals.

YOU CAN DO IT.

This technique also directs your attention towards **future outcomes** (say, the final goal of finishing your book, losing weight and keeping it off, quitting smoking). These future outcomes are valuable in themselves. They are valuable because they are of **personal benefit**.

Highlighting accrued success also helps you change your focus, and increases satisfaction. When you achieve something difficult, or something that takes a long time, then your satisfaction is much stronger than if it is immediate gratification. And not only do you feel satisfaction, you justifiably can feel **proud** of yourself. [95]

Finally, as you repeat the behaviour, then, as we discussed in the earlier chapters, it becomes automatic, and easier, and more intuitive---and before you know it, you have beaten your bad habit or created your new habit.

CHAPTER 8 WHEN THINGS GO WRONG

"There is only one day left, always starting over: it is given to us at dawn and taken away from us at dusk."
Jean-Paul Sartre

But of course, life doesn't work in a nice linear way, even if I describe it in this way. No matter how motivated you are---you are almost guaranteed to lapse. Sorry if you are perfect, it's just that I'm not---about a million miles from perfection whatever that might be. Indeed, I often say to people, 'I strive for adequacy'.

So how do you stop (or at least reduce) lapses?

Analyse (don't criticise)

Stuff ups are almost guaranteed. You might have a goal to not to drink during the week, but then you have a horrendous day at work, and get stuck in a traffic jam on the way home, and then the kids are playing up more than usual---so you just grab a glass of wine and collapse in front of the TV.

Then, the next morning, **you feel terribly guilty**. Unfortunately most of us want to everything perfect every time, and for things to happen quickly.

We have been programmed this way by the media, to seek some impossible perfection. We read articles about some celebrity, whose pictures are airbrushed and Photoshopped anyway, who is mega rich and has a personal chef and their own trainer, whose job depends on them looking a certain way, and we think that we can do the same thing as they do (even though they probably don't do it at all, and what we see is a carefully crafted advert).

However, the problem with most of us, is that if we fail one day at a minor goal, we tend to think that we are going to fail at the whole goal. That is why it is so common that if we break a diet, be it alcohol or food, then we often go on a huge binge---and give up the diet.

One reason for this is that we have too high expectations of ourselves; that we are **perfectionists.**

Another reason is that we beat up on ourselves; we are often our own worst **critics**. When we fail, we are really mean to ourselves. Imagine if we spoke to other people like we spoke to ourselves. We'd have no friends. Everyone would think we were total a-holes.

Well, that is what all the negative talk does to our mind. We are constantly telling ourselves that we are bad, we cannot stick to our goals, we are useless, fat, alcoholics (or whatever nasty things we say to ourselves, either aloud or in our minds).

Negative self-talk is incredibly psychologically damaging, and is in itself a bad habit. Perhaps that is the habit that we need to break first, BEFORE our other habits? Think about it.

In Buddhism, they call self-criticism 'the second arrow'. The first arrow is the thing you have done, whether it is to drink or eat too much, forget to exercise, yell at the children or any of a million other ways that we behave and that we don't like our behaviour. That is the first arrow that enters our body. The **second arrow** is when we beat ourselves up about our slip, so we are compounding our pain by adding new pain.

You can never change the past. You can only change the future.

Also, think about it; since when do we immediately learn a new skill? It takes ages to learn new skills (especially for me, indeed, in my mid-50s, I'm STILL trying to learn how to dance, and I suspect I never will dance in any way that does not result in suppressed laughter, or worse, pity, from those around me).

Just remember when you were learning to drive, or to ride a bicycle; did you start off knowing what to do, having an instant ability? Of course not. Well, some of us might have, but I think it is highly unlikely.

Instead, what we did was try and try and try and fail, and one day, we would just ride our bike, or drive our car, and not even think about it. It has become a HABIT.

Here's a great quote from a substance disorder website, **"LAPSES DO NOT HAVE TO BE RELAPSES."**

So, don't criticise yourself, but do analyse your slipup. And you can use many of the techniques referred to in the earlier chapters.

Honestly look back at the slip up and ask: What were the circumstances? How was I feeling? Was I bored/irritated/angry/depressed/not thinking?

How to deal with cravings[96]

But, what about cravings? What do I do about them? If you are trying to give up something, then you need to deal with the craving. Did you know that a craving only lasts about 7 minutes at the most? Can you distract yourself for that hideously long period of time? I've got a great solution to deal with the craving to spend time on social media or to snack or to have a drink of wine---I play Sudoku on my IPad. Sure, it's still electronic, but it is fiendishly difficult (because I play the 'expert' games), and it really distracts me. Also, the cat likes to sit on my chest, and I feel guilty getting up to get a snack, and she then begs for food, which is annoying.

A good one to do with food and alcohol is to go and clean your teeth or chew some gum. Toothpaste and chewing gum make booze and food taste disgusting, and then you have to clean your teeth again. During the day, go outside and do some exercise, or weed the garden. Getting your hands dirty is wonderfully relaxing, and you won't want to snack with filthy hands (well, I hope not), or traipse dirt into the house, making a nice little path to the fridge.

Finally, don't keep the offending drink or food in the house. If you cannot resist wine or chocolate or soda, then don't buy any. Generally, a craving won't last as long as it takes to drive or walk to the shops!

Another solution to cravings, if you are not trying to give up completely, is to **give in to them**---but only once, and not to feel guilty if you. What do I mean? Well, sometimes I crave really odd foods, for example that horrible multi-coloured sugar encrusted popcorn that you normally only get in the shops before Christmas. Oh dear, now I feel like having some!

However, if I give in and buy a packet of the offending stuff, I cannot just let it sit in the cupboard and eat a bit at a time. No, I eat half a packet, or even more. So what I do, is to eat the stuff. As much as I want---but nothing else. If I want to eat an entire packet of sugary popcorn, then I do. Afterwards, I feel sick. And I don't eat any more---until the next time. I literally eat coloured popcorn once a year.

Now of course, some of you might find eating an entire packet of popcorn quite nice, and something you can do more than once a year---in that case, don't deny yourself the popcorn, or chocolate or whatever---but eat a little--- and do it mindfully.

I spoke of mindfulness earlier in the book, but it basically just means to be aware and mindful of what you are doing. Habits and mindfulness are diametric opposites. The very meaning of habit is to do something **mindLESSly.**

Consistency

Importantly, it's not essential that you practice the new habit/ stick to your goal absolutely 100%. Many people start a new regime, dieting, giving up smoking, exercise, etc., and when they lapse, then they give it all up. It's really common that dieters will stick rigidly to their diet for days or weeks, and then something will happen, and they will lapse, and eat something they shouldn't, or even go on a binge. When that happens, it's common that the person feels extreme guilt, and quite often, will behave in the complete opposite to the control of the past few days or weeks.

But psychological research shows that it's not necessary to stick to your new behaviour all the time. Indeed, you only need to perform the behaviour about 75-80% of the time to create a new habit. This is why some new diets, such as the alternate day fasting diet, or the 5:2 intermittent fasting diet, can work so well. You are not expected to stick to the diet every day, and on the off days, can eat as much as you like, what you like.

Good luck!

YOU CAN DO IT ☺

APPENDICES

APPENDIX 1 RESOURCES

TESTS

Are you actually drinking too much? Here are some online tests to give you some indication of this.

- https://www.drinkaware.co.uk/selfassessment
- https://www.yourdrinkingprofile.com.au/
- http://www.euro.who.int/en/health-topics/disease-prevention/alcohol-use/do-you-drink-too-much-test-your-own-alcohol-consumption-with-the-audit-test

How to identify bad habits?

- http://www.audreymarlene-lifecoach.com/bad-habits.html
- https://snack-girl.com/snack/identify-bad-habits/
- http://www.adeledurand.com/how-to-identify-a-bad-habit/
- https://breakingmuscle.com/fitness/theres-no-such-thing-as-willpower-how-to-identify-triggers-of-bad-habits

Habit breaking and Mindfulness Apps and sites

- https://qz.com/269930/a-cornell-scientist-came-up-with-four-ways-to-lose-weight-without-dieting/?utm_source=qzfbarchive
- https://insighttimer.com/
- https://www.fastcompany.com/3033523/5-free-apps-for-making-good-habits-and-breaking-bad-ones
- https://www.imore.com/best-habit-makingbreaking-apps-set-you-right-path-new-year

REFERENCES

NIH, 2012. Breaking bad habits, why it's so hard to change. Online http://newsinhealth.nih.gov/issue/jan2012/feature1

Dean, J. 2012. Automatic Drive: How Unconscious Cognitive Biases Help Fire Our Motivation. Online http://www.spring.org.uk/2012/07/automatic-drive-how-unconscious-cognitive-biases-help-fire-our-motivation.php

Cherry, K. 2016. The Nervous System and Endocrine System. Online http://psychology.about.com/od/biopsychology/p/NervousSystem.htm

Zevenbergen, T. 2012. Why Humans Are Hard-Wired to Run. Online http://blogs.theprovince.com/2012/05/24/why-humans-are-hard-wired-to-run/

---

[1] Dachis, A. 2012. How Seinfeld's Productivity Secret Fixed My Procrastination Problem. Online https://www.lifehacker.com.au/2012/02/how-seinfelds-productivity-secret-fixed-my-procrastination-problem/

[2] Wikipedia, nd. André the Giant. Online https://en.wikipedia.org/wiki/Andr%C3%A9_the_Giant

[3] Whitehouse, D. 2003. 'Fake alcohol' can make you tipsy. http://news.bbc.co.uk/2/hi/health/3035442.stm

[4] Wikipedia. nd. History of alcoholic drinks https://en.wikipedia.org/wiki/History_of_alcoholic_drinks

[5] Goldman, J.G. 2014. Do animals like drugs and alcohol? http://www.bbc.com/future/story/20140528-do-animals-take-drugs

[6] World Health Organisation. 2014. Is harmful use of alcohol a public health problem? http://www.who.int/features/qa/66/en/

[7] Drinkwise. nd. Tips to help you drink properly. https://drinkwise.org.au/drinking-and-you/tips-to-help-you-drink-properly/#

[8] Australian Government Department of Health. nd. The Australian Standard Drink. http://www.alcohol.gov.au/internet/alcohol/publishing.nsf/Content/standard

[9] Balranald Club website: http://www.balranaldclub.com.au/130-2/standard-drink-rtd/

[10] Adapted from Alcohol.org.nz. nd. What happens when you drink alcohol? http://www.alcohol.org.nz/alcohol-its-effects/about-alcohol/what-happens-when-you-drink-alcohol

[11] Adapted from NIH. nd. Alcohol Overdose: The Dangers of Drinking Too Much https://pubs.niaaa.nih.gov/publications/alcoholoverdosefactsheet/overdosefact.htm

[12] Addictionblog.org website http://alcohol.addictionblog.org

[13] Friedman, L.F. 2015. The things most likely to kill you in one infographic. Business Insider. https://www.businessinsider.com.au/the-things-most-likely-to-kill-you-in-one-infographic-2015-2?r=US&IR=T

[14] Lygouris G, Figueredo VM. Alcohol and arrhythmias. OA Alcohol 2014 Jan 18;2(1):2. http://www.oapublishinglondon.com/article/1222

BREAKING THE BOOZE HABIT

[15] NIH. 2015. Beyond Hangovers: understanding alcohol's impact on your health. https://pubs.niaaa.nih.gov/publications/Hangovers/beyondHangovers.pdf
[16] Meadows, G.G. and Zhang, H., 2015. Effects of Alcohol on Tumor Growth, Metastasis, Immune Response, and Host Survival. Alcohol research: current reviews, 37(2), pp.311-322. https://www.ncbi.nlm.nih.gov/pmc/articles/PMC4590626/
[17] http://www.medscape.com/viewarticle/499247
[18] James, L. 2017. Alcohol and weight gain. http://lucasjamespersonaltraining.com/alcohol-weight-gain-infographic/4180/
[19] Hensrud, D. nd. Is too little sleep a cause of weight gain? http://www.mayoclinic.org/healthy-lifestyle/adult-health/expert-answers/sleep-and-weight-gain/faq-20058198
[20] Mann, D. 2013. Alcohol and a Good Night's Sleep Don't Mix http://www.webmd.com/sleep-disorders/news/20130118/alcohol-sleep#1
[21] NIH. 2004. ALCOHOL'S DAMAGING EFFECTS ON THE BRAIN. https://pubs.niaaa.nih.gov/publications/aa63/aa63.htm
[22] Wikipedia. nd. Selective Serotonin Reuptake Inhibitor. https://en.wikipedia.org/wiki/Selective_serotonin_reuptake_inhibitor
[23] NIH. 2012. The Link Between Stress and Alcohol. https://pubs.niaaa.nih.gov/publications/AA85/AA85.htm
[24] Wikipedia. nd. Alcohol and cortisol. https://en.wikipedia.org/wiki/Alcohol_and_cortisol
[25] Samson, H.H. and Harris, R.A., 1992. Neurobiology of alcohol abuse. Trends in Pharmacological Sciences, 13, pp.206-211.
[26] Ramesh Shivani, M.D., R. Jeffrey Goldsmith, M.D., and Robert M. Anthenelli, M.D. 2002. Alcoholism and Psychiatric Disorders https://pubs.niaaa.nih.gov/publications/arh26-2/90-98.htm
[27] The Costa Rica News. 2017. The Spiritual Consequences of Alcohol Consumption http://thecostaricanews.com/spiritual-consequences-alcohol-consumption/
[28] Sutherlin, E. 2017. Moderate drinking improves heart health? Genes say 'not so fast'. https://geneticliteracyproject.org/2017/01/13/moderate-drinking-improves-heart-health-genes-say-not-fast/
[29] Sharma, A. nd. Habit Formation: Basis, Types and Measures for Effective Habit Formation http://www.psychologydiscussion.net/habits/habit-formation-basis-types-and-measures-for-effective-habit-formation/638
[30] Darwin Awards. nd. http://www.darwinawards.com/darwin/
[31] Paul, M. 2013. The Love Hormone is Two-Faced http://www.northwestern.edu/newscenter/stories/2013/07/the-love-hormone-is-two-faced.html
[32] Jabr, F. 2012. Does Thinking Really Hard Burn More Calories? http://www.scientificamerican.com/article/thinking-hard-calories/
[33] Swaminathan, N. 2008. Why does the brain need so much power. http://www.scientificamerican.com/article/why-does-the-brain-need-s/
[34] Layton, J. nd. Is it true that if you do anything for three weeks it will become a habit? http://science.howstuffworks.com/life/form-a-habit.htm
[35] Wikipedia. nd. Hebbian Theory. https://en.wikipedia.org/wiki/Hebbian_theory
[36] Wikipedia. nd. Procedural Memory. https://en.wikipedia.org/wiki/Procedural_memory
[37] Marley, J. 2017. The Amazing World of Psychiatry: A Psychiatry Blog. The anterior

cingulate cortex. https://theamazingworldofpsychiatry.wordpress.com/tag/anterior-cingulate-cortex/
[38] http://www.sciencedirect.com/science/article/pii/S0896627315001336
[39] Wikipedia. nd. Orbitofrontal cortex. http://en.wikipedia.org/wiki/Orbitofrontal_cortex
[40] Wohl, S. 2011. The Experience of Eating http://www.yalescientific.org/2011/04/the-experience-of-eating/
[41] Scharwtz, J. 2015. The neuroscience of habit with Dr Jeffrey Schwartz http://www.happyandwell.com.au/neuroscience-habit-dr-jeffrey-schwartz
[42] Gillan, C.M. and Robbins, T.W., 2014. Goal-directed learning and obsessive–compulsive disorder. Phil. Trans. R. Soc. B, 369(1655), p.20130475. https://www.ncbi.nlm.nih.gov/pmc/articles/PMC4186229/
[43] Gillan, C.M. and Robbins, T.W., 2014
[44] Wikipedia. nd. Dorsolateral prefontal cortex. http://en.wikipedia.org/wiki/Dorsolateral_prefrontal_cortex
[45] Gillan, C.M. and Robbins, T.W., 2014
[46] Wohl, S. 2011. The Experience of Eating http://www.yalescientific.org/2011/04/the-experience-of-eating/
[47] Tamplin, H. 2017. The Experience of Eating http://metro.co.uk/2017/06/20/man-feared-dead-after-trying-to-have-sex-with-crocodile-is-probably-fake-news-6721235/
[48] http://onlinelibrary.wiley.com/doi/10.1002/ejsp.674/full
[49] Lally, P., Van Jaarsveld, C.H., Potts, H.W. and Wardle, J., 2010. How are habits formed: Modelling habit formation in the real world. European journal of social psychology, 40(6), pp.998-1009. https://www.ncbi.nlm.nih.gov/pmc/articles/PMC3505409/
[50] Gardner, B., 2015. A review and analysis of the use of 'habit' in understanding, predicting and influencing health-related behaviour. Health Psychology Review, 9(3), pp.277-295. http://www.tandfonline.com/doi/pdf/10.1080/17437199.2013.876238
[51] Wikipedia. nd. Automaticity. http://en.wikipedia.org/wiki/Automaticity
[52] Orbell, S. and Verplanken, B., 2010. The automatic component of habit in health behavior: habit as cue-contingent automaticity. Health psychology, 29(4), p375.
[53] Being Human. 2013. Conscious Thought. Am I Thinking What I'm Thinking? http://www.beinghuman.org/article/conscious-thought
[54] Gardner, B., 2015. A review and analysis of the use of 'habit' in understanding, predicting and influencing health-related behaviour. Health Psychology Review, 9(3), pp.277-295.
[55] Gardner, B., 2015. A review and analysis of the use of 'habit' in understanding, predicting and influencing health-related behaviour. Health Psychology Review, 9(3), pp.277-295.
[56] Verplanken, B. and Wood, W., 2006. Interventions to break and create consumer habits. Journal of Public Policy & Marketing, 25(1), pp.90-103. Verplanken and Wood
[57] Verplanken, B. and Wood, W., 2006. Interventions to break and create consumer habits. Journal of Public Policy & Marketing, 25(1), pp.90-103. Verplanken and Wood
[58] Lam, S.P., 1999. Predicting intentions to conserve water from the theory of planned behavior, perceived moral obligation, and perceived water right. Journal of

Applied Social Psychology, 29(5), pp.1058-1071.

[59] Carreon, M. 2013. This Bra Lets You Smuggle Booze (and Gives You Bigger Boobs) http://www.laweekly.com/music/this-bra-lets-you-smuggle-booze-and-gives-you-bigger-boobs-4167944

[60] Galiani, S. Can incentives improve our habits? http://blogs.iadb.org/desarrolloefectivo_en/2014/07/01/can-incentives-improve-habits/

[61] Ruiter, Robert AC, Charles Abraham, and Gerjo Kok. "Scary warnings and rational precautions: A review of the psychology of fear appeals." Psychology and Health 16, no. 6 (2001): 613-630

[62] Layton, J. nd. How Fear Works http://science.howstuffworks.com/life/fear1.htm

[63] Shove, E. (2003). Comfort, cleanliness and convenience: The social organization of normality (Vol. 810). Oxford: Berg.

[64] Wikipedia. nd. Death of Elisa Lam. https://en.wikipedia.org/wiki/Death_of_Elisa_Lam

[65] http://science.sciencemag.org/content/162/3859/1243

[66] Quinn, J.M., Pascoe, A., Wood, W. and Neal, D.T., 2010. Can't control yourself? Monitor those bad habits. Personality and Social Psychology Bulletin, 36(4), pp.499-511. Quinn, J.M., Pascoe, A., Wood, W. and Neal, D.T., 2010. Can't control yourself? Monitor those bad habits. Personality and Social Psychology Bulletin, 36(4), pp.499-511. http://www-ccd.usc.edu/assets/sites/545/docs/Wendy_Wood_Research_Articles/Habits/quinn.pascoe.wood.neal.2010_Cant_control_yourself.pdf

[67] Psyblog. 2010. How to Banish Bad Habits and Control Temptations http://www.spring.org.uk/2010/07/how-to-banish-bad-habits-and-control-temptations.php

[68] Quinn, J.M., Pascoe, A., Wood, W. and Neal, D.T., 2010. Can't control yourself? Monitor those bad habits. Personality and Social Psychology Bulletin, 36(4), pp.499-511.

[69] http://www.mindful.org/the-science-of-mindfulness/

[70] Zarbock, Gerhard, Ringer, Silka, Ammann, Axel, Lynch, Siobhan, 2015

[71] Siegel, D. J. 2010. The Science of Mindfulness http://greatergood.berkeley.edu/topic/mindfulness/definition

[72] Duval, M. 2011. Introduction to Mindful Eating by Michelle DuVal / The Mindful Center https://www.youtube.com/watch?v=6tw93IgfL0U

[73] Lally, P. and Gardner, B., 2013. Promoting habit formation. Health Psychology Review, 7(sup1), pp.S137-S158. Lally and Gardner; Verplanken, B. and Wood, W., 2006. Interventions to break and create consumer habits. Journal of Public Policy & Marketing, 25(1), pp.90-103. Verplanken and Wood

[74] Moderation Management. nd. http://www.moderation.org/

[75] Lally, P. and Gardner, B., 2013. Promoting habit formation. Health Psychology Review, 7(sup1), pp.S137-S158. Lally and Gardner; Verplanken, B. and Wood, W., 2006. Interventions to break and create consumer habits. Journal of Public Policy & Marketing, 25(1), pp.90-103. Verplanken and Wood

[76] Thomas Friedrichsmeier a,⇑, Ellen Matthies c,1, Christian A. Klöckner

[77] Comrades Marathon. nd. http://comrades.com/

[78] Parkrun. nd. http://www.parkrun.com.au/

BREAKING THE BOOZE HABIT

[79] Lally, P. and Gardner, B., 2013. Promoting habit formation. Health Psychology Review, 7(sup1), pp.S137-S158.
[80] Layton, J. nd. Is it true that if you do anything for three weeks it will become a habit? http://science.howstuffworks.com/life/form-a-habit.htm
[81] Psyblog. 2009. How Long to Form a Habit? http://www.spring.org.uk/2009/09/how-long-to-form-a-habit.php
[82] Popova, M. 2014. How Long It Takes to Form a New Habit http://www.brainpickings.org/index.php/2014/01/02/how-long-it-takes-to-form-a-new-habit/
[83] Daniel M. Bernstein, Cara Laney, Erin K. Morris, Elizabeth F. Loftus (2005). False Memories About Food Can Lead to Food Avoidance. Social Cognition: Vol. 23, Special Issue: Autobiographical Memory: Empirical Applications, pp. 11-34. http://guilfordjournals.com/doi/abs/10.1521/soco.23.1.11.59195
[84] Laney, C. 2014. It's Shockingly Easy to Create False Memories http://www.thedailybeast.com/articles/2014/02/09/it-s-shockingly-easy-to-create-false-memories.html
[85] Pomeroy, S.R. 2013. How to Instill False Memories http://blogs.scientificamerican.com/guest-blog/how-to-instill-false-memories/
[86] Estrella, M. 2014 How a Password Changed My Life http://www.huffingtonpost.com/mauricio-estrella/how-a-password-changed-my-life_b_5567161.html
[87] My FitnessPal. https://www.myfitnesspal.com/
[88] My FitnessPal https://www.myfitnesspal.com/
[89] Lee, C.D., Chae, J., Schap, T.E., Kerr, D.A., Delp, E.J., Ebert, D.S. and Boushey, C.J., 2012. Comparison of known food weights with image-based portion-size automated estimation and adolescents' self-reported portion size. Journal of diabetes science and technology, 6(2), pp.428-434. http://www.ncbi.nlm.nih.gov/pmc/articles/PMC3380789/
[90] Duhigg, C. How Habits Work. From The Power of Habit. http://charlesduhigg.com/how-habits-work/
[91] Smart Water Bottle. https://hidratespark.com/
[92] Cherry, K. 2017. What Is Cognitive Dissonance? http://psychology.about.com/od/cognitivepsychology/f/dissonance.htm
[93] Keohane, J. 2010. How facts backfire Researchers discover a surprising threat to democracy: our brains. http://archive.boston.com/bostonglobe/ideas/articles/2010/07/11/how_facts_backfire/
[94] Wikipedia. nd. Geologic Time Scale https://en.wikipedia.org/wiki/Geologic_time_scale
[95] Lally and Burke, Swigart, Turk, Derro, & Ewing, 2009
[96] Lifehacker. 2014. Hack your brain to use cravings to your ad advantage. http://lifehacker.com/5887614/hack-your-brain-to-use-cravings-to-your-advantage

Printed in Great Britain
by Amazon